CLASSIC SERMONS ON SPIRITUAL WARFARE

Compiled by

Warren W. Wiersbe

kregel PUBLICATIONS

Grand Rapids, MI 49501

Classic Sermons on Spiritual Warfare, compiled by Warren
W. Wiersbe. © 1992 by Kregel Publications, a division of
Kregel, Inc., P. O. Box 2607, Grand Rapids, MI 49501. All
rights reserved.

Cover Photo: Art Jacobs
Cover Design: Alan G. Hartman

Library of Congress Cataloging-in-Publication Data

Classic Sermons on Spiritual Warfare / compiled by Warren
W. Wiersbe.
    p.   cm.— (Kregel classic sermons series)
Includes biographical references and index.

    1. Spiritual warfare—Sermons. 2. Sermons, English.
I. Wiersbe, Warren W. II. Series: Kregel classic sermons
series.

BV4509.5.C53   1992   235'.4—dc20   92-13765
                                    CIP

ISBN   0-8254-4049-1 (pbk.)

1 2 3 4 5 Printing/Year 96 95 94 93 92

Printed in the United States of America

CONTENTS

SCRIPTURE TEXT INDEX

PREFACE

THE *KREGEL CLASSIC SERMONS SERIES* is an attempt to assemble and publish meaningful sermons from master preachers about significant themes.

These are *sermons*, not essays or chapters taken from books about themes. Not all of these sermons could be called "great," but all of them are *meaningful*. They apply the truths of the Bible to the needs of the human heart, which is something that all effective preaching must do.

While some are better known than others, all of the preachers, whose sermons I have selected, had important ministries and were highly respected in their day. The fact that a sermon is included in this volume does not mean that either the compiler or the publisher agrees with or endorses everything that the man did, preached, or wrote. The sermon is here because it has a valued contribution to make.

These are sermons about *significant* themes. The pulpit is no place to play with trivia. The preacher has thirty minutes in which to help mend broken hearts, change defeated lives, and save lost souls; and he can never accomplish this demanding ministry by distributing homiletical tidbits. In these difficult days we do not need "clever" pulpiteers who discuss the times; we need dedicated ambassadors who will preach the eternities.

The reading of these sermons can enrich your own spiritual life. The studying of them can enrich your own skills as an interpreter and expounder of God's truth. However God uses these sermons in your own life and ministry, my prayer is that His Church around the world will be encouraged and strengthened.

WARREN W. WIERSBE

The Weapons of Our Warfare

William Culbertson (1905-1971) was born and educated in Philadelphia and was identified all of his ministry with the Reformed Episcopal Church of America. He pastored churches in Pennsylvania and New Jersey and in 1937 was elected Bishop of the New York and Philadelphia Synod. In 1942 he became Dean of Education at the Moody Bible Institute in Chicago; and in 1947 he was named Acting President upon the death of Will H. Houghton. In 1948 he became president of the school, a position he held with distinction until 1971 when he was named Chancellor. "My first impression and the lasting one," said Dr. Wilbur M. Smith, "is that he is a man of God." He was in great demand as a preacher and widely recognized as a leader in Christian education.

This sermon comes from the compilation of his Moody Bible Institute "Founder's Week" messages *The Faith Once Delivered*, published in 1972 by Moody Press, and is used by permission.

William Culbertson

1

THE WEAPONS OF OUR WARFARE

IT IS ON MY HEART to speak on the theme, "The Weapons of Our Warfare."

There is a general recognition that these are ominous days. The great increase of knowledge is paralleled only by man's inability to harness it, so that we seem to be sitting on an atomic bomb that may explode momentarily. Somewhere I heard the story that when evangelist Billy Graham was ushered into the presence of Winston Churchill before the latter retired from active service, the great prime minister greeted him with this plaintive question: "Young man, is there any hope?"

Our world is a world of secularism, materialism, moral breakdown, international chicanery and conflict. Our own nation knows immorality in the forms of drunkenness, robbery, arson, sexual deviation, adultery, lawlessness, unbelief. These are dangerous days. These are days when courts hand down decisions which protect the rights of criminals over the rights of society. These are days when churchmen have denied the Book, traduced the Lord, endorsed sin, and now wonder why conditions are as they are. The Word of God is plain: "They sow the wind, and they shall reap the whirlwind" (Hosea 8:7). Indeed, the text for our day may be well be: "Because iniquity [lawlessness] shall be multiplied, the love of the many shall wax cold" (Matt. 24:12).

What shall we do? We do not decry "positive action." We acknowledge the need for the worthwhileness of proper legislation, civil defense, police effort to fight crime. We do not oppose legal investigations. We do not oppose the efforts of good men to find panaceas. But what is our basic duty as Bible-believing Christians? What are we to do? There is injustice. There is mounting crime. There is a

7

terrifying turning from things just decent, let alone the higher ethic of Christianity. Lawlessness is abroad. Fear grips many hearts. What are we to do? Are we to parade? Are we to demonstrate? Are we to get into politics? Are we to set up lobbies in Washington? Are we to do all we can within the law to protest wrong and champion the right? Whatever may be said for such activities, let us remember that these are not our chief weapons. They are not our strongest weapons. They are not our best weapons.

It seems to me that we need to remind ourselves that our chief enemy is not a man. And it is not a group of men. It is not a human organization. It is not an inimical "ism" that is our chief foe. Our chief foe is Satan, and his powers of darkness. "Put on the whole armor of God, that ye may be able to stand against the wiles of the devil. For our wrestling is not against flesh and blood, but against the principalities, against the powers, against the world-rulers of the darkness, against the spiritual hosts of wickedness in the heavenly places" (Eph. 6:11-12). The conflict of the ages is going on. And let me observe that what is behind the lawlessness and moral breakdown in the world today is satanic in origin. Frankly, the Bible teaches that seducing and teaching spirits and demons are to lead men astray in later times (1 Tim. 4:1). Our weapons, therefore, cannot be of this world. Buildings, worldly success, wealth, worldly acclaim, earthly authority will not avail. Our weapons have to be spiritual.

There is a parenthesis in 2 Corinthians 10 that goes to the heart of the matter and establishes the principle to which I would like to address myself now. Verse 3 reads: "For though we walk in the flesh, we do not war according to the flesh," and then verse 4 continues and is a parenthesis: "(for the weapons of our warfare are not of the flesh, but mighty before God to the casting down of strongholds)." We propose, then, to think with you of these weapons of our warfare which are not carnal but which are mighty, to the pulling down of stongholds.

What are our secret weapons? What can we lay hold of in order to make the greatest contribution, not only to the welfare of the church but to the well-being of society as well? I take it that there are at least six such weapons God has put at our disposal. It is not my purpose to deal exhaustively with these, but I should like to mention them, for all of us need reminding of these things. In what I shall say there is nothing new. But I think I shall be mentioning things that have been largely forgotten.

The Power of Prayer

The first of these weapons of our warfare is the power of prayer. James 5:17-18 tells us: "Elijah was a man of like passions with us, and he prayed fervently that it might not rain; and it rained not on the earth for three years and six months. And he prayed again; and the heaven gave rain." If you have a marginal reference Bible you may see that a more literal translation of "he prayed fervently" is that "he prayed with prayer." I think the translators have gained the idea of that repetition, "prayed with prayer," for it denotes completion; it denotes fervency; it denotes earnestness; it denotes a literal laying hold of God. These are not simply words falling from Elijah's lips. These were words that tumbled over his lips from Elijah's lips. These were words that tumbled over his lips from a fervent, warm heart that knew and loved God and believed that God heard and answered prayer. Elijah prayed with prayer.

I have given tribute on other occasions to the book on prayer that helped me most in my early ministry, *The Power of Prayer*, by a former leader of Moody Bible Institute, Dr. Reuben Archer Torrey. I have been reading it again, and I came to a passage comparatively early in the book I couldn't pass by. I want to read it for you now because it humbled me before God, it spoke deeply to my own soul about my own desperate need to learn to pray. Listen to these words from Dr. Torrey:

"I believe that the devil stands and looks at the Church today and laughs in his sleeve, as he sees how its members depend upon their own scheming and powers of organization and skillfully devised machinery. 'Ha, ha,' he laughs, 'you may have . . . your costly church edifices and your fifty-thousand dollar church organs, and your brilliant university-bred preachers, and your high-priced choirs, and your gifted sopranos, and altos, and tenors, and basses, and your wonderful quartets, your immense men's Bible classes, yes, and your Bible conferences, and your Bible institutes, and your special evangelistic services, all you please of them, it does not in the least trouble me, if you will only leave out of them the power of the Lord God Almighty sought and obtained by the earnest, persistent, believing prayer that will not take 'no' for an answer'."

"Prayer has as much power today," writes Dr. Torrey, "when men and women are themselves on praying ground and meeting the conditions of prevailing prayer, as it ever has had." Has God spoken to you recently about this matter of praying with prayer? Or have you been so occupied with things temporal, so seeking after outward demonstration of success, that the place of prayer is cold and empty?

Periodically God has spoken to my heart again and again from certain texts of Scriptures. As I prepared to speak to you this morning, I asked Him to speak to me again from these passages. Listen to Isaiah 64:7: "There is none that calleth upon thy name, that stirreth up himself to take hold of thee." Oh, how God has excoriated this cold heart of mine about my prayerlessness with that text. For, you see, prayer doesn't come easily and naturally, and it isn't something we like to do in our fleshly natures. We have to stir up ourselves. And we have to mean business to lay hold.

Along with that verse I think of Acts 6:4 where the early disciples said, "We will give ourselves continually to prayer" (KJV). We'll give ourselves. It takes a bit of doing. It isn't something that comes automatically. We'll give ourselves— with purpose of heart, with determination. We'll give ourselves to prayer. Ephesians 6:18: "With all prayer and supplication praying at all seasons in the Spirit, and watching thereunto in all perseverance and supplication." And linked with that verse is Jude 20: "praying in the Holy Spirit." I remember hearing something like this: "We may be beaten in the conflict. We may be worsted in the battle. Our faces may be plunged in the dust of defeat, because of the power of the adversary and the greatness of Satan, but we're not beaten yet! For we can still lay hold of what John

Bunyan used to call 'all prayer.'" And that's what Ephesians 6:18 is talking about—with all prayer and supplication, at all seasons, in the Spirit.

The simplest definition of praying in the Spirit came to me years ago from a great Bible teacher in the East, who said, "We pray in the Spirit when the Holy Spirit prays in us." When there is yieldedness to Him, when there is obedience to Him, when there is faith in God, when we are praying in the will of God—that's praying in the Spirit of God. And I think of our Lord's words in Luke 18:1 that men "ought always to pray, and not to faint." Let me go back to Dr. Torrey and leave this first weapon with a comment from him: "Prayer brings the power of God into our work." And I say, "Amen." We cannot have too much prayer, but, alas and alack, too frequently we have too little.

The Power of Godly Living

There is a second weapon that God has put at our disposal—the power of godly living. "Ye are the salt of the earth," said the Lord Jesus. A scene comes to my mind that is related in Genesis 18. Three men traveling in the Holy Land were approaching the city of Hebron. They came to the plains of Mamre where Abraham had set up his tent, and an incident occurred there after Abraham had fed them. Before they left, they said, "Shall we not share with Abraham the thing which God is about to do?" And they evidently told him of the impending destruction of Sodom and Gomorrah.

Abraham undoubtedly thought of Lot and his family and began to speak to God. You know the story. "Peradventure there are fifty righteous within the city: wilt thou consume and not spare the place?" (v. 24). And God answered, "If I find . . . fifty righteous . . . I will spare all the place for their sake" (v. 26). Fifty righteous souls would have meant deliverance from the judgment of God about to fall on that wicked city. But that's not the end, for Abraham kept up his plea, and he went from fifty to forty. And from forty to thirty. And from thirty to twenty. And from twenty to ten. And God said, "I will not destroy it for the ten's sake" (v. 32).

Do you see that this passage is telling us that in the economy and government of God, He will withhold judgment if there are those who are righteous within the place where judgment is to be poured out. Do you see that if there had been ten righteous souls in Sodom and Gomorrah, they would have meant more to those cities than all their standing armies and all the acumen and strategy of their generals? And it is my judgment that holy men and holy women who know and love God, whose names have never sounded in the halls of any congress, or any parliament, have done more to sustain nations than the armies thereof.

But there may come a day when even the righteous in a land will not hold back that land from judgment. Listen to this. This is an overpowering word. "Son of man, when a land sinneth against me by committing a trespass, and I stretch out my hand upon it, and break the staff of the bread thereof, and send famine upon it, and cut off from it man and beast; though these three men, Noah, Daniel, and Job, were in it, they should deliver but their own souls by their righteousness, said the Lord Jehovah" (Ezek. 14:13-140. And look at verse 20: "Though Noah, Daniel, and Job, were in it, as I live, saith the Lord Jehovah, they should deliver neither son nor daughter; they should but deliver their own souls by their righteousness."

There will come the day, and one wonders whether it may not be coming very soon, for the nations of the earth today, when judgment will fall. Certainly when the Lord comes for His own, and those who know and love the Lord are caught up together in clouds to meet Him in the air, the time of dire and awful judgment will begin. But until that day, when in the purposes of God it is God's action to bring judgment without remedy, the righteous are the salt of the earth. This is a weapon. It's a great weapon. It's a weapon that speaks to the hearts of sinners. It's a weapon that brings a sense of the presence of God and gives courage to the Christian. "Ye are the salt of the earth." McCheyne wrote: "A holy minister is an awful weapon in the hand of God."

The Power of Faith

Weapon number three is the power of faith. For, says the Word of God, "without faith it is impossible to be well-pleasing unto Him." We stand in a terrifying day. But that is no reason to be discouraged. That is no reason to seek out some place where we may hide ourselves and await the coming holocaust. Let us dare to believe God. Listen to these verses from which God has been speaking to me. James 1:6-8: "Let him ask in faith, nothing doubting: . . . let not that man think that he shall receive anything of the Lord; a double-minded man, unstable in all his ways." Mark 9:23: "All things are possible to him that believeth." And Mark 11:22: "Have faith in God." That last text was paraphrased by Hudson Taylor: "Hold God's faithfulness."

Whatever the earthly scene, you and I can, in absolute trust in God, go forward. Let us dare to believe God—that God will yet honor His word; that God will yet vindicate His saints; that God will yet, according to His program, bring in the universal reign of righteousness and truth when His Son comes again. So, thank God, we can believe God. And I really think that the harder it is to believe, the better God likes it, and the greater He will reward it. So, let's dare to hold onto our faithful God.

The Power of Truth

The fourth weapon is the power of truth. Said the Lord Jesus in His high-priestly prayer, "Thy word is truth." Let's think of this for a moment. What was it the Lord Jesus had said? You'll find it in John 8:32: "Ye shall know the truth, and the truth shall make you free." Truth has power to deliver from error—from error about God and self and Satan and the hereafter. Truth also has power to deliver from the dominion of sin. There is a self-contained power in the truth of God that vibrates with delivering life. That's one of the reasons we should hide it in our hearts. It not only is good advice; it's great power. Isn't that a striking word Paul uses in 2 Corinthians 13:8: "We can do nothing against the truth, but for the truth." And that's true. In an ultimate sense, when all is done, when all is finished, when the whole course is wound up, truth is going to emerge victorious. And nothing and no one can hold it back. The Word of God will be vindicated.

Frankly, I don't think it takes any ingenuity for a simplehearted child of God, reading the Word of God, to see that the truth of God as to the course of this age is moving on just as God said it would. I remember my teachers years ago saying that in the last days false teachers would arise, speaking evil things. And so I say to my dear Christian friends, the train's on time, the schedule's right, and we're moving inexorably to the final triumph. The weapon of the power of prayer, the weapon of the power of godly living, the weapon of faith, the weapon of truth.

The Power of Love

Let us mention the weapon of the power of love. Galatians 5:6 speaks of "faith working through love." Oh, the power of love. "Now abideth faith, hope, love, these three; and the greatest of these is love" (1 Cor. 13:13). Because of the bitterness of the adversary, because of the cruelty of the circumstances through which you have to move, has your heart shriveled up in malice and bitterness and hatred? Where is the love among us? I am not speaking of condoning sin. Not for one moment would I crown unbelief as worthy. But I still believe it's possible to love men who are actually their own greatest enemies. And so the Word of God reads, "If a man says, I love God, and hateth his brother, he is a liar" (1 John 4:20). Now that's as direct preaching as I think I've ever heard. And the verse goes on: "He that loveth not his brother whom he hath seen, cannot love God whom he hath not seen." Oh, that we would know the presence of the Spirit of God in such a heartwarming manner that, despite some differences— not the difference of unbelief and belief but the differences between those who are truly God's children—we might be overcome in love. I know of nothing that is more calculated to be a weapon in our hands than to love our foes. "Love your enemies, do good to them that hate you" (Luke 6:27). May God give us to know how to love.

The Power of Hope

But there's a final word—the power of hope. This is a great weapon God has given us. For hope isn't a weak, namby-pamby word. Its true meaning is not reflected in the way it has come to be used in the twentieth century. It's a strong word. It means something that I expect with my whole heart. And not only do I expect it, it's what I desire above everything else. Hope! And God has given us hope. "Now the God of hope fill you with all joy and peace in believing, that ye may abound in hope, in the power of the Holy Spirit" (Rom. 15:13). And so there is hope for us.

You ask, "With all that's going on in the world, how can you be hopeful?" And I answer you, "As a child of God, having the Word of God, How can I be hopeless?" Hopeful we should be. For you see, we have God's present protection. And not only so, we have both God's present control and His future reign. For 1 Corinthians 15:25 says, "He must reign."

So, very simply, God has given us some weapons which are not carnal, but which are mighty, which are able to pull down strongholds. And I believe that as you and I mean business with God and lay hold of prayer and consecration and faith and truth and love and hope, we'll begin to wield the weapons that will count for God. The weapons of our warfare are not carnal, but are mighty, to the casting down of strongholds. Let us use them by the power of the Spirit.

Valiant in the Fight

Alan Ogle Redpath (1907-1989) was born in England and trained to be a chartered accountant. Converted to Christ as a young man, he immediately became involved in evangelism and was greatly used of God in youth crusades and city-wide meetings. He pastored the Duke Street Church, Richmond, from 1940 to 1953. Crowds were so great that in 1947 they moved the services into a local movie theater. He was a regular speaker at the British Keswick Convention as well as in conferences overseas. He pastored the Moody Church, Chicago, from 1953 to 1962, and the Charlotte Chapel, Edinburgh, from 1962 to 1966. From 1966 on, he was associated with the Capernwray Fellowship and taught at their school in Lancaster. He was the author of ten books.

This sermon was taken from *The Making of a Man of God*, published in 1962 by Fleming H. Revell, and used by permission.

Alan Ogle Redpath

2

VALIANT IN THE FIGHT

2 Samuel 23:1-39

EPHESIANS 6:13 IN THE WEYMOUTH TRANSLATION reads: "Therefore, put on the complete armor of God, so that you may be able to stand your ground in the evil day, and having fought to the end, to remain victor in the field."

We hear from all over the world something of the pressures and problems of missionary service today. Everywhere on the mission fields tensions are increasing. Some have their source in the demand of nations for independence and freedom. In most places missionary personnel is barely adequate to maintain present positions, quite unable to extend the message to the uttermost parts of the earth to hasten the coming of the King. Missionaries also have their own individual burdens: problems of ill health, incompatibility on the field, lack of supplies, and personal spiritual battles.

It is impossible, therefore, for us to regard the mission fields of the world as far-off places which are detached from our own personal life and Christian ministry at home. Missionary service is not one thing over there, and the place of service that we occupy here something quite different. The field is the world, and it is more than ever "one world." As we think of the tremendous responsibility that confronts the church in this missionary task, what is the answer to all the problems and difficulties? I am perfectly sure that the basic need is not just more money, or more equipment, or even more missionary recruits—the answer is on a deeper level than that altogether.

Wherever we may be placed in the will of God, in whatever circumstances we find ourselves, each Christian is a fort of resistance in the name of heaven against all the forces of evil in the world today. When the church is complete and Jesus comes to take to Himself His body, the church, then the world will know the agony of evil which is unresisted by the presence of the people of God. But today the Christian stands in the name of the Lord wherever he is, as a point of resistance to the enemy of righteousness. He doesn't stand alone; he is one of a great army, that company of people who have been redeemed by the precious blood and who share together the life of their Lord, although scattered in different parts of the world.

The triumph of the church as a whole depends upon the personal victory of every Christian. In other words, your victory, your life, your personal testimony, are important to the cause of God today. What happens out in New Guinea, down in the Amazon jungle, over in disturbed Congo, is not unrelated to what happens in your own personal relationship with God and your personal battle against the forces of darkness. Victory for the church on the whole world-front depends upon victory in your life and in mine; "home" and "foreign" situations cannot be detached.

Three Heroes in David's Army

Therefore the answer is not, I repeat, in more money, more equipment, more people; but it is in dedication, commitment, abandonment to God. This we find illustrated by three outstanding men among David's army.

At this point in the story we are looking back from a high peak. David the King, although for a time rejected, had returned and was administering his kingdom. In 2 Samuel 23 are listed the names of the men who stood with him through thick and thin, men who were identified with him at any cost.

We will mention just three of them. The first was Adino, who slew eight hundred of the enemy on his own (2 Sam. 23:8). Another was Eleazar who, when the people of God were in rout and confusion, defied the Philistines to the point of complete weariness until, when the battle was over, he could not unclasp his fingers from his sword (2 Sam. 23:9-10). The third, Shammah, stood his ground against an attack of the enemy, defended it, and slew the Philistines (2 Sam. 23:11).

These men won victories which had some common factors. In each case it was victory against overwhelming odds. It was victory in the face of utter exhaustion. It was victory when the people of God were in confusion and retreat. It was victory that was won only in the power of the Lord, for we read in two places, "The Lord wrought a great victory that day" (2 Sam. 23:10, 12).

Jeremiah said, "I cannot hold my peace [can find no peace], because thou hast heard, O my soul, the sound of the trumpet, the alarm of war" (Jer. 4:19). I believe that the whole missionary enterprise in this century is at stake until we have this Old Testament illustration (which is amplified in New Testament truth in Ephesians 6:13) translated into twentieth-century experience, not only in the lives of a few missionaries in Borneo or South America or Africa, but in the lives of every ransomed soul. There must be the same spirit of dedication in the face of overwhelming odds, in the face of confusion in the ranks of the people of God who are so often in retreat, in the face of absolute physical and mental and often spiritual exhaustion. In the face of all these things we must be able to stand our ground and to remain victor in the field, to be able to say, "The Lord hath wrought a great victory this day!"

But this, I repeat, should be not simply Old Testament history, but your experience and mine in the personal spiritual battles of our lives.

Heroes of Today

I think of one of our missionary families in the New Guinea battle line with the problems of Bible translation into the language of the tribes-people. Another couple, in Southeast Asia, after repeated physical setbacks are again working at the task of getting the Word of God into the language of their people. I think of an elderly missionary, deprived of his loved ones and refusing to retire, spending his last years on the field, and of another couple who have spent their lives in Africa—if you ask them when they will retire, they retort, "Only when we get to heaven!" Another couple, who have served in South America for nearly forty years, first in evangelism, then teaching, followed by a Bible Institute ministry, are now confirming the local churches, traveling ceaselessly to strengthen believers in the Lord.

We receive letters that tell of overwhelming odds, of absolute exhaustion, of weariness of mind, weariness of soul, weariness of body. I begin to ask myself, "What do we know of a life on that level of sacrifice?" Victory in those key battle fronts depends upon victory in your life and mine right now where we are today.

In order to reinforce this truth, let me draw from Ephesians 6. Here Paul writes to the Christians of his day to tell them of a position that must be maintained: "that ye may be able to stand." In other words, where I am in the will of God, in my circumstances, I am to stand my ground.

It was for this purpose that the Lord Jesus Christ threw Himself into the battle on our behalf. Without Him we were not only down, we were conquered and helpless. But now, "being justified by faith, we have peace with God through our Lord Jesus Christ: By whom also we have access by faith into this grace wherein we stand" (Rom. 5:1-2).

The power of the cross in a man's life puts him on his feet and enables him to stand in this evil day. Without God and without salvation he was down and helpless, but the Lord has come and lifted him up and set his feet on the Rock. In the spiritual battles that come upon a man of God who is dedicated to the will of God, he is called upon never to flinch, but to stand firm against the adversary in the power of Jesus Christ our Lord.

Is that position being maintained? Are we standing our ground against the enemy of our souls? This is illustrated in the life of Shammah who, in the midst of a Philistine raid, when the people of God were running helter-skelter from the enemy, stood his ground and defied them until he had slain so many that they had to retreat.

Ephesians 6 says not only that we must stand our ground, but that we must wrestle. Our enemy is not flesh and blood, but "the world rulers of this darkness" and "the spiritual hosts of wickedness in the heavenly places" (6:12, ASV). Every man of God is engaged somewhere in the depths of his soul in a spiritual battle. There he has to fight with everything he possesses, not only to maintain his stand (in the passive sense) but, as Paul emphasizes, to wrestle. This is the language of personal conflict, toe to toe with the enemy of our souls to resist evil in the name of the Lord.

It is quite easy for Christian people somehow to avoid the sense of battle and conflict and to take their ease. "Woe to them that are at ease in Zion," says Amos 6:1. Many of us quite readily become so occupied with material things and with our work that it is a long time since we really fought a battle against sin alone on our knees. How much do I really know, and how much do you know, about prayer that resists the powers of darkness and refuses to give in? Have I spent half an hour alone each day this week on my knees in prayer like this? Have you?

Our prayer life, our whole spiritual witness, can lose its priority and become mechanical so that it has no flavor of life or conflict in it at all. Yet victory on the whole battle-front depends upon maintaining our position in the name of the Lord Jesus, so that when the enemy flings his fiery darts, we wrestle and stand our ground. By God's grace, we fight and refuse to give in.

Where Are You in the Battle?

Are you engaged in this spiritual warfare? Are you standing your ground? In your home life, in your personal walk with God, in your prayer life, in your testimony and witness among your colleagues at the office and your family at home, are you standing your ground today? In the position where God has put you, are you resisting the enemy or are you in retreat? Have you said, concerning missionary service, "If I pay my pledge, that is all that is required of me. If I write a letter occasionally, that is all I am expected to do. But as for the impact of spiritual warfare upon my soul, I know nothing of that—in fact, I have kept clear of it! It is surely only for the few"? No, no, this is a position to be maintained by us all.

The Christian's Armor

Paul speaks further of a provision that has been made

in order that we may stand our ground. "Wherefore take unto you the whole armor of God, that ye may be able to withstand" (Eph. 6:13). Let us look briefly at this armor which God has provided in Jesus Christ to enable the child of God to stand. Here are the details of the power by which we may resist the devil.

Paul mentions first the girdle of truth about our loins: in other words, a man's strength derives from his character of godliness and truthfulness. He speaks of the breastplate of righteousness, which indicates a conscience void of offense before God and man, a rightness of life and conduct that relates a man's belief to his behavior. The shoes of preparedness make feet ready to run errands for the King of kings, ready to follow the Master wherever He may lead, ready to obey His commands and spread the message of the gospel—next door or anywhere for Jesus.

Speaking of the shield of faith, Paul says it is "above all." I have no doubt but that as he was describing this armor he had his eye upon the Roman soldier who guarded him in the prison from which this letter was written. He saw the great shield that reached from the man's neck almost to his feet, covering his body entirely. This part of the Christian's armor is his complete confidence in the ability of the Lord Jesus to defeat the enemy. Then there was vital protection in the helmet of salvation, and divine power in the sword of the Spirit.

I observe, as I am sure you have, that there is no armor for the back of the Christian, no provision for running away from the enemy. It is all for the front and the head: retreat is not considered a possibility for the child of God. He is to stand his ground.

There is only one offensive weapon, the sword of the Spirit. All else is for defense, for security against the attacks of the enemy; the Christian is given only the sword of the Spirit, the Word of God, for subduing the enemy.

I would remind you that this armor was forged by the Lord Jesus Christ. That is why He came, that is why He lives to make intercession for us today. When He entered into Jerusalem the word was, "Behold, thy King cometh!" At Bethlehem, at Nazareth, in Judea, in Galilee, at Calvary, from the door of the open tomb, He forged this armor for His people. The Bible tells us that "the weapons of our warfare are not carnal, but mighty through God to the pulling down of strong holds" (2 Cor. 10:4).

May I say that one of the greatest perils for us as individual Christians in this day is not simply that we neglect the armor and try to escape the spiritual battle, looking upon the missionary as a unique specimen who faces it in distant lands; one of the greatest perils of our time is that we substitute for heaven's armor something of our own imagination. I could sum up all the pieces of this armor that we have been talking about in one word: character. The very character of the Lamb of God, His integrity and righteousness, purity and holiness, faith and salvation, is the sum of it. Character is the armor that God supplies, and in place of it the church tends to substitute equipment, gimmicks, money, and all kinds of other things in order that somehow it might make an impact upon our day and generation. We have forgotten that our weapons are *not* carnal, but spiritual. However, if we claim and use them, they *are* mighty through God to the pulling down of the strongholds of Satan.

God has made provision in Jesus Christ to enable you to stand your ground right where you are, in your immediate circumstances. Our armor is not outward things, not material equipment or money or anything like that. It is character, the godliness and righteousness and loveliness and sweetness and grace—the very life of Jesus Christ imparted to you and me so that we may be equipped to wield the sword of the Spirit for Him.

No man can use his Bible with power unless he has the character of Jesus in his heart. No man can have impact for God through the use of Scripture in preaching, teaching, or witnessing, if to him it is merely a textbook. His life must be filled with the very life of Jesus Christ. Our offensive weapon depends upon our wearing all the defensive armor; the power to attack depends upon being completely equipped for defense against Satan with every bit of the character of our Lord Jesus. If we are to maintain our position in this evil day, if we are to fight through to the end and remain victor on the field, then we must put on the whole armor of God. If we wear it, then we are able to wield the sword of the Spirit in the power of God.

This is the provision that heaven has made, for it is "not by might, nor by power, but by my spirit, saith the Lord of hosts" (Zech. 4:6). Jesus stooped from the throne to the cross in order that He might forge for us a complete armor of His holy character.

There is one other supremely important thing that I must say here, for if you would understand the secret of victory in your own life, there is a Person whom you must meet.

The Armor Is Christ

When the Lord Jesus gives us this armor, He is not giving us something apart from Himself. The armor is Christ—not simply His blessings, not just righteousness or truth or faith or salvation or the sword of the Spirit. It is not these apart from Him, but Christ Himself. Paul said also, "Put ye on the Lord Jesus Christ, and make not provision for the flesh, to fulfill the lusts thereof" (Rom. 13:14).

All the wealth that is in our wonderful Savior, of which Satan tries to rob us, all our personal walk with God from which Satan tries to drag us away, and all the victory we need in the welfare, is in the Person of our living Lord from whom Satan tries to keep us separated so that he can defeat us.

I have a serious question to ask you: Have you really met God in Jesus Christ at this level? Do not let that question slip by, because I am persuaded that one reason for our lack of dedication and devotion to the missionary call, and often our lack of ability to stand and win through where we are in the name of the Lord, is because we have not really met God in Jesus Christ like this.

When Joshua had crossed the River Jordan with the people of God, he went out for a walk to survey the first great city that stood in his way, Jericho. As he looked at its battlements, no doubt calculating his resources and how he could use them to overcome this mighty obstacle which he dared not leave in the rear, which had to be attacked and possessed—suddenly he encountered a man with a drawn sword in his hand. Joshua challenged him, "Art thou for us, or for our adversaries?" (Josh. 5:13).

Joshua and Jesus

The answer came from this One who was none other than the Lord Jesus Christ Himself, who often appeared in this way in the Old Testament: "Nay; but as captain of the host of the Lord am I now come." Immediately Joshua fell on his face before Him asking, "What saith my Lord unto his servant?" This mysterious Commander, the living God, answered him, "Loose thy shoe from off thy foot; for the place whereon thou standest is holy" (Josh. 5:15).

On that day the leader of God's people in his day met God in Jesus Christ at a new level. He saw Him as one whose sword was drawn in His hand, whose very presence was holy ground.

What a poor illustration is the story of Eleazar, who fought through one day against the Philistines to the point of absolute exhaustion, so that he could not unclasp his fingers from his sword! What a pale reflection he is of the One who stood by Jericho with a sword in His hand, and who has never, never withdrawn His hand from the battle since He won it for us at Calvary! He imparts His authority to men like Joshua, who meet Him at a new level and recognize that the responsibility of the battle is not their own but God's.

It was not a question of what resources or equipment Joshua had, or the numerical strength of his people. The situation was under the control of the Captain of an invisible host who could defeat any strategy of the enemy. Joshua gladly handed over the battle entirely to Him.

The word came to Joshua, as it had to Moses, that the ground whereon he stood was holy. As a matter of fact, Joshua was on his face in worship and surrender. But the man who is on his face before God is always standing against the enemy. It is only the man who has met God in Christ, whose heart has been broken at the cross, who has been brought on his face before the Lord, who can stand before the enemy.

If I try to stand before God in my own puny self-righteousness, in self-confidence and arrogance, thinking that I have equipment that can see me through to a life of victory, then I shall fall before the devil. But if I fall before the Lord, I find that I am enabled to stand before the enemy.

I trust that you have come to see that the whole missionary enterprise scattered throughout the world today, with its problems, testings, suffering, shortage of manpower and material and finance, is that way because Christian people in the homelands have not met God in Jesus Christ like that. God is calling, not simply for more money, greater response, more recruits—He is calling for men and women who will fall before Him in surrender that they might stand before the enemy. What is your position today?

NOTES

The Course and End of Satan's World System

Robert Thomas Ketcham (1889-1978) was converted to Christ in 1910 and began pastoring the First Baptist Church, Roulette, Pennsylvania, in 1912. A self-taught man with a profound grasp of Bible truth, he pastored churches in Pennsylvania, Ohio, Indiana, and Iowa, and in 1932 was one of the founders of the General Association of Regular Baptist Churches. He was president of that fellowship for three years and in 1948 was named National Representative, serving in that office until 1960, when he became National Consultant. Ketcham was highly respected as a Bible expositor, conference speaker and a crusader against modernism and for the fundamentals of the faith.

This message is taken from *The Death Hymn of Christ and Other Sermons*, published in 1966 by the Regular Baptist Press, and is used with their permission.

Robert Thomas Ketcham

3

THE COURSE AND END OF SATAN'S WORLD SYSTEM

TO MAKE THE ANNOUNCEMENT that Satan is managing the affairs of this world is at once to arouse interest and, in many instances, bitter antagonism. To say that this whole world system in which we are living is under the control and domination of Satan will startle some people. It seems on the surface, to deny the sovereignty of God, so opposition immediately arises before the opponent has really thought his way through. Think with me now, and I am sure you will see that my statement is not a wild, fanatical one. It is based upon Scripture itself, and evidenced by observation of history as it unfolds.

That Satan is the god of this world, that he does have managerial abilities and operations over the affairs of the world, is evidenced many times in the New Testament as well as the Old. One or two observations will suffice to settle that point. You will recall that in the record of the temptation of Jesus (better translated the *testing* of Jesus), Satan appeared to Him, and at one point in the series of testings said he would give Him all the kingdoms of the world if He would worship him. He caused them to pass before Him in panoramic vision. All the kingdoms in all of their glory Satan offered to Him if He would worship him. In our delight at the forthright renunciation by our Lord of the whole proposition, and our happy realization that He did not fail and could not fail, there is a little line in the picture which we too often overlook completely. At no point in the rebuttal of Jesus that day did He deny that Satan had a *right* to offer the kingdoms to Him. Or perhaps putting it in better form, at no point did He enter a protest to Satan's claim of ownership. Satan showed Him the kingdoms of the world, and he said, "I will give them to you." Thereby, he claimed control over them. They are his system. They are his kingdom. Jesus Christ did not deny the validity of Satan's claim to the management of the affairs of this world. He had rebuffed the temptation, but He did not rebuke the tempter on the basis that he was offering something to which he had no claim.

In John 12 He said, "Now is the judgment of this world: now shall the prince of this world be cast out" (v. 31). So Satan again, from the lips of the Lord, was called the prince of this world.

Satan's Vow

Paul called him "the prince of the power of the air" and the "god of this world." It is not within the function or scope of this message, therefore we must not spend our time going into it, but it would be interesting to go into the origin of this individual whom we now know as Satan. So many passages in the Old Testament are clear that, as a created being, he was a great angel prince. Very evidently it was this world of ours, spinning in space, over which God set Lucifer, the son of the morning, to rule. He was to rule it for God and for His glory, but pride came into his heart, and he said, " . . . I will ascend into heaven, I will exalt my throne above the stars of God: I will sit also upon the mount of the congregation, in the sides of the north: I will ascend above the heights of the clouds; I will be like the most High" (Isa. 14:13,14; cf. Ezek. 28:12-14). This was his declaration of rebellion. There cannot be two who are "most" High. If there is one most High there cannot be another at the same time. When Satan said, "I will be like the most High," it was the announcement that he was intending to put God out of business, pull Him down from His throne and take over His government. It was there that sin was born and the son of the morning became the old serpent which is called the Devil.

Now, there are many Scriptures which teach us that rulership over this planet has not yet been taken out of the hands of the usurper. He is still permitted to run the affairs of this world. If you want to know why, you will have to wait until you see God and ask Him. He knows why He is permitting it. But one of these days the permission will run out, and things will be different. Just what God's great purposes are in the time of the power of the usurper, I do not fully know, but He knows, and I wait for the unfolding of those purposes as time moves toward eternity. I am perfectly content to let them rest in the hand of a sovereign God. We are amazed at the silence of God in the face of the operations of the prince of this world—the god of this age—the Devil—Satan—the old serpent.

Time was, back yonder in the Old Testament, when God spoke, but it is now nearly two thousand years since His voice has been heard. Two thousand years ago God opened the heavens and said, "This is my beloved Son: hear him," and the heavens have been as silent as brass since then. Wave after wave of persecution and martyrdom have swept over God's people, apparently unnoticed by God. Men have been at the stake, torn to pieces, beheaded at the block, torn by wild beasts, and killed by beastly men. God's people have been killed all the day long, boiled in oil, fried on gridirons, sharp sticks and knives run under their fingernails, eyes gouged out with sharp sticks. They have been tortured with red-hot pincers on the way to the headsman's block, and all of it apparently unnoticed by God. And we ask, "Why doesn't God speak?"

The "Silence of God"?

Some have gone so far as to assume that the silence of God is an indication of His impotence. In their minds, God has been reduced to a being of divine sentimentality sitting out there on a cloud somewhere, looking down upon a world that has gone berserk with sin, wringing His hands in distress and despair, saying, "It's out of my hands and my control. The Devil has won and I can't do anything about it." So they have assumed that the silence of God is an indication of impotence.

Let me tell you something, dear friend. The silence of God is not the silence of *impotence*. As Dr. H. O. Van

Gilder, Sr., has pointed out, the silence of God these two thousand years is the silence of *omnipotence*. God doesn't have to get excited and in a dither and run up and down Hallelujah Avenue, wringing His hands and calling special cabinet meetings of the heavenly hosts because somebody has gone berserk down here on earth. He does not have to do that. Nobody has to do that except the person who knows that the situation is out of hand and there isn't anything that can be done about it.

But the individual who knows that regardless of how far a thing seems to be out of hand, that when He is ready all He has to do is speak and the thing will be changed, does not have to become excited. God is sitting in the heavens silent—not because He is impotent. When His purposes are fulfilled, the day of the usurper will be over.

You have a picture of this thing I am talking about in the Books of Samuel, Kings and Chronicles. Israel wanted a king. God said, "You can't have a king, I'm your king." They said, "Well, we want to be like other nations. We want a king we can see." And so they came coaxing, and finally God said, "All right, I will give you a king, but I will send leanness to your soul. I will give you what you want but you must take the consequences." So Saul was set as king over Israel, and for a while he did a fair job of reigning and ruling for God. Then he got on the toboggan slide of sin and landed clear at the end of it in the tent of a little old fortune teller. From there he went out to the battlefield where God said, "This is enough. Let him fall on his sword."

God's Chosen King—David

In the meantime, while all of this was taking place, He had officially set Saul aside and anointed David to be king. David was the real king, but he was the king in exile. He was the king rejected. He was the king despised. He was the king hunted and hounded by the usurper upon the throne. During his rejection, when he lived in the hills and the holes and the caves of the forest, from time to time men of Benjamin's and Judah's tribes and others broke with Saul and his kingdom and his system.

They went outside the camp and identified themselves with the one whom they knew to be the true king, although he was not yet on the throne. They shared his privations and his sufferings.

Then one day the usurper was dealt with, and Saul came to his end. Out of these forests and caves there came a little, bedraggled band with David marching at its head. The men of the tribes of Israel who had broken with the usurper and had shared the privation and suffering with the true king outside the camp came marching back with him. Flags were flying; hosannas and hallelujahs to the king were heard everywhere. All Israel was happy, but the happiest in the whole multitude were the men from the tribes who had broken with the old system and had known what it was to live outside the camp with a rejected king. They had lived subject to all the dangers of such a life because they had gone out and said, "David, thine we are and on thy side, thou son of Jesse." All those who had suffered with him were now coming back to reign with him! Why did God let all of this happen? I do not know. Why He let the usurper, Saul, sit upon the throne after He had officially denied him the right to do so, while His own king suffered out in the forest, I don't know. But God knew.

Why does He now let the usurper, Satan, whom He has officially set aside as the king of this world, still hold sway while His King, Whom He has anointed—His own Son, King Jesus, still walks outside the camp of this world? I do not know, but He knows, and that is good enough for me.

God's True King

These are not the days when King Jesus is marching through the world receiving its acclaim. These are the days of His rejection. He is still outside the camp of the world and, tragically, is still outside the camp of great sections of the professing church. One of these days, however, the shout of "Bring back the King" will be heard and out of the forests of Glory He will come! What a happy day for this poor world so long under the heel of the usurper. And how unspeakably happy those who through the centuries since His rejection have, like the tribes of ancient Israel, identified themselves with God's *true* King. They have broken with Satan and his system and have gone out to become subjects of another King. They share His reproach and sufferings while they wait for His glory. The happiest crowd of all the universe in the day of His coming will be those who thus suffered and who are now coming with their conquering King to reign. So much for the Old Testament picture of a New Testament truth.

The Ultimate End of Satan

Now I would like to ask a question as to where Satan belongs. Matthew 25:41 says, " . . . Depart from Me, ye cursed, into everlasting fire, prepared for the devil and his angels." The Lord Jesus says the ultimate end of Satan is the lake of fire. We are told about that place in Isaiah 30:33: "For Tophet is ordained of old; yea, for the king it is prepared; he hath made it deep and large: the pile thereof is fire and much wood; the breath of the Lord, like a stream of brimstone, doth kindle it."

So often we have heard it said by modernists, who deny the reality of Hell, that there could be no such thing as an *eternal* lake of fire because there would not be combustible material enough in the universe to keep a fire going forever. If these poor men only knew that the fire of Hell is not generated or maintained by combustible material of any kind, it would help them to understand. Let us look for a few minutes at the matter of fire and the holiness of God.

In Deuteronomy 4:24 and Hebrews 12:29 we read, "For our God is a consuming fire." Again and again in the Scriptures, God is revealed as expressing His holiness in the form of literal fire. Sometimes this expression of holiness is in *condemnation* of sin. At other times it is in *commendation* of righteousness. On the one hand God manifests His displeasure with sin in the form of literal fire. On the other hand He manifests His *pleasure* with righteousness in the form of literal fire.

For instance, in the case of Sodom and Gomorrah, we are told that the wickedness of these cities had increased so that the cry of it had reached into Heaven, and God

announced that He was coming down to destroy. When
He did so come, it was in the form of *literal fire.* Consider
the case of Nadab and Abihu (Lev. 10). When these two
men offered strange fire before the Lord, fire came out
from the presence of the Lord and devoured them. God's
holiness was expressed in the form of literal fire.

Condemnation or Commendation?

On the other hand, we find instances such as Elijah on
Mount Carmel, where God expressed His *delight* in the
form of fire. On Mount Carmel, God's holiness leaped
forth in the form of literal fire, and consumed Elijah's
offering in commendation and vindication of the righteous
position of the prophet. On the day of Pentecost, God's
holiness was manifested in tongues of literal fire resting
upon every believer, as was promised in Matthew 3:11.
Thus we see that fire is a symbol of God's holiness, acting
in one direction or the other. It either *condemns* or *com-
mends.* It causes either *perishing* or *purging.*

The question immediately arises: What makes the difference? Why should the holiness of God condemn in one
instance and commend in another? The answer is the
presence or absence of sacrificial blood. In the case of
Sodom and Gomorrah there was no blood; therefore, condemnation. In the case of Nabad and Abihu there was no
blood; therefore, condemnation. In the case of Elijah there
was the whole burnt offering; therefore, commendation.
In the case of the one hundred and twenty in the upper
room there was blood; therefore, commendation.

Perhaps one of the most outstanding illustrations of
the principle we are trying to make clear is found in
Isaiah 6:1-8. The prophet was standing in the temple
area at the hour of the evening sacrifice when he saw the
Lord. He at once fell on his face and cried, "I am a man of
unclean lips. . . ." Whereupon a seraph took a coal from off
the altar, drew it across Isaiah's lips and said, "Thine
iniquity is taken away, and thy sin purged." It is interesting to note that this coal came from the brazen altar.

In Leviticus 9:24 we read that the fire on the altar was
kindled directly from God. God's holiness had expressed

itself in the kindling of the fire on the brazen altar where sin was to be dealt with. In Leviticus 6:12,13 we read that this fire was never to go out. Therefore the fire on the altar, in every sense of the word, was God's fire. It was for failure to recognize this that Nadab and Abihu got into trouble when they thought they could produce better fire. (Incidentally, the modernists will do well to take warning as they parade around with their strange fire.) It was the hour of the evening sacrifice; therefore the coals on the brazen altar at that moment were coals of God's fire, but coals which had been touched by the drippings of sacrificial blood. The result was that when God's fire, God's holiness, touched the lips of Isaiah, it resulted in purging and cleansing. Had this coal been taken from the altar where there had been no sacrificial blood applied, Isaiah would have been utterly consumed. Our God is a consuming fire. *He consumes either the sin or the sinner.* The presence or absence of sacrificial blood determines which it shall be.

The holiness of God is pursuing every poor, lost sinner today. Sooner or later it will overtake him and the fate of Sodom and Gomorrah, Nadab and Abihu, will result *unless* that poor, lost sinner pleads the blood of Jesus Christ as his shelter, whereupon the holiness of God will be turned into a cleansing, purging agent, and he, like Isaiah, will hear, "Thine iniquity is taken away, and thy sin purged."

The Fire of God

I have been asked hundreds of times if I believe the fire of Hell to be literal. Let me answer that question with Isaiah 30:33. I quote from the American Standard Version: "For a Tophet [place of fire] is prepared of old; yea, for the king it is made ready; he hath made it deep and large; the pile thereof is fire and much wood; the breath of Jehovah, like a stream of brimstone, doth kindle it." It is the eternal holiness of God, expressing itself in condemnation of sin. How did He express that hatred of sin in Sodom and Gomorrah? *By literal fire.* How did He express it in the case of Nadab and Abihu? *By literal fire.* How will He express it through the ceaseless ages of an endless eternity? *By literal fire.* The fire of hell is the absolute holiness of God expressing itself in literal fire, in its eternal condemnation of sin. Thus we see that the fire is not fed by combustible and perishable material. It is as eternal as God.

It is here that Satan belongs. And we see him in that place in Revelation 20:10: "And the devil that deceived them was cast into the lake of fire and brimstone . . . and shall be tormented day and night forever and ever."

The question is, Where is he now? According to Jehovah's Witnesses, he is bound and has been since 1914. Well, I am sure that whoever is running things while Satan is bound is certainly doing a good job of it!

Walking in the World

Where is he now? Let us see. "Now there was a day when the sons of God came to present themselves before the Lord, and Satan came also among them. And the Lord said unto Satan, Whence comest thou? Then Satan answered the Lord, and said, From going to and fro in the earth, and from walking up and down in it" (Job 1:6,7). That is one place he is found. He is walking up and down in the earth and going to and fro in it, and apparently has some kind of access into the presence of God. Is it always to be so?

Revelation 12:7-10 says, "And there was war in heaven. . . . And the great dragon was cast out, that old serpent, called the Devil, and Satan, which deceiveth the whole world. . . . And I heard a loud voice saying in heaven, Now is come salvation, and strength, and the kingdom of our God, and the power of His Christ: for the accuser of our brethren is cast down, which accused them before our God day and night."

Now these Scriptures in their simplicity indicate: (1) Satan is not now in Hell; (2) he has access to the earth personally; (3) he has some strange access, or at least communication, with God; (4) his work on earth is that of deceiving, and (5) he is the accuser of the brethren.

Satan's Master Plan

We have the deceptive work of Satan itemized in particular in many, many Scriptures, but we want to look at it in general just now. *Satan's master plan is to achieve in this world the best possible conditions that can be obtained apart from God.* Let me say that again. Satan's master plan is to achieve in this world, here and now, the best possible conditions that can be obtained apart from God. I am not altogether sure that Satan is pleased with such raw, revolting sin as we see engulfing the world. Not that he is at all sorry about the victims, but I think these are people who have gone even farther in open sin than he would wish, and the world and the flesh have taken over and are running rampant.

I have found, after more than fifty years of preaching the gospel, that it is much easier to win a drunkard or a harlot to Jesus Christ than it is to win a moral man to Him. When that drunkard staggers into my study, or the woman with the scarlet past comes and wants to find the way out of trouble, I know why. It is because they are so low down they have to reach up to touch bottom. They know they need something. They know they have tried with their last little bit of self-respect and self-will; their little bag of tricks is empty. They are ready to cast themselves upon Christ. The hardest men I have ever had to deal with in all these years of soul-winning are the men who are so confident in their own goodness and their own morality that they think they do not need a Savior.

Satan does not care how good you are. In fact, the more moral the better. And he does not care how religious you are. In fact, the more religious the better. If you stop just short of becoming a Christian, you are his big success. Notice I have said, "The best possible conditions that can be obtained *apart from God*." In the light of this assertion, let us examine the first temptation that Satan applied to our race.

Satan and Adam

You will find the record of it in Genesis 3:1-7. I would remind you that it was not a temptation to *deliberate degeneration and debauchery*. You see, we have the habit of associating everything that is vile and dirty and repulsive with Satan. I will grant you that when he caused the race to fall, that in that fallen nature there are the seeds of all of his debauchery and degeneracy. But I do not think Satan wants too much of that to be evidenced, as I have already indicated. At least his first temptation to our father and mother, Adam and Eve, certainly did not indicate it. He did not tempt Adam to run away with some other woman. He had the only one there was. It was a temptation to *self-improvement through the acquisition of knowledge.* He argued something like this: "You say the Lord God said you couldn't eat of that fruit, that tree of knowledge of good and evil? Well, do you know why? Do you know why He forbade you to eat of that tree of the knowledge of good and evil? If you do—you will know as much as He does, and that would not suit Him. Let me tell you something, Lady Eve. It would be a good thing if you and your husband would just take a good meal off that tree. Then you would know what God knows—good and evil."

That is not a temptation to get drunk or rob a bank. That is a temptation to make something out of yourself by the acquisition of knowledge, *but a knowledge which had to be obtained apart from God,* for God had said, "Ye shall not eat of it." When we disobey God we are on our own and apart from God. We are in opposition to God. So the first temptation was the temptation to self-improvement through the acquisition of knowledge, but I repeat for emphasis' sake, a knowledge which was to be obtained apart from God.

A good result—a desirable thing—is the acquisition of knowledge and self-improvement, but not when reached by a wicked method. It was to be done apart from God. And that is still Satan's program in our educational systems, from the grade school on up through the universities. Get all the knowledge you can, but do not let God determine its character and content.

God—or Evolution?

I was in a Michigan city some time ago when a high school professor said to a class of 150 pupils, "Of course, you know I don't believe there is a God. All I've got to say is if there is one, Satan must have something on Him the way He's letting him run things." The tragedy involved in that, as deep and terrible and awful as the statement itself, was that not one solitary Christian father or preacher in that city ever raised a voice in protest.

The whole evolutionary hypothesis is based upon the principle we are here discussing, namely, the acquisition of knowledge apart from God. They want to find out about origins. They want to know about creation. They want to know how they got here. So they propose hypotheses of how creation started and how this whole complex universe came about. They come to the Scriptures and read the straightforward declaration that God created all things by a fiat act. Why not take that if they want the truth? There is not a scientist on the face of the earth that I know anything about who will say that evolution is a proved fact. They all admit that it is only theory. They admit that there is no bona fide evidence of evolution, and then turn around and teach our children that that is how we got here!

Why will not this intellectual group we call scientists accept the simple, provable, and manifestly sensible Bible record of creation? I will tell you why. There is another record involved in the first two chapters of Genesis. It is the record of human sin, divine judgment and blood atonement. Man sinned and God judged him in the person of a slain Lamb. The old unregenerate heart will not agree to nor accept this. These so-called scientists see that most plausible explanation of the origin of the universe and all of its species as set forth in the simple, straight forward statements of Genesis, but they deny it. Why? *Because if they admit the truth concerning creation, they will have to admit the truth set forth in the same chapters that man is a sinner and God is holy, and that the only way for the two to get together is by the blood of a slain Lamb.* This they will not admit, so they continue their search for knowledge. But they must pursue it apart from God.

Note for just a moment the detailed working of this first move to Satan. When he tempted our first parents to gain this knowledge, there was only one thing that stood in the way of attaining it, namely, *a divine command.* Under the force of plausible reasoning, that restraint was overcome. How did he do it? God's wisdom and love in imposing such a command in the first place were called into question. Satan's implied argument to Eve was, "Now, look, you say He said you mustn't eat of the tree of the knowledge of good and evil?" Eve replied, "Yes, He said that and I must not even touch it." She lost her case when she said that. God had not said she couldn't *touch* it. He had only forbidden her to *eat* it.

This adding to the Word of God by Eve was significant. It evidenced the fact that she was afraid to stand on the Word alone. She must add something to it in order to strengthen it. Satan knew at once that his scheme was working. She was already doubting God. He followed up his advantage by insinuating that God did not love her. It is as though he had said, "Look, Eve, God knows that in the day that you eat of that you will know as much as He does." Now what is the implication involved in that? The bare, bald implication is that if God loved Eve so much, then why would He withhold that wonderful blessing from her?

The First Higher Critic

So His voice and His wisdom in imposing the restriction were brought into question. Man that day set himself to do what he has been prone to do ever since, namely, *to question and pass judgment upon the expediency, love and justice of a divine command.* There in the garden, the first higher critic was born. That is Satan's method down to this hour. Let us not be too hard on Eve and Adam for falling for Satan's subtle, implied argument which brought into question God's love and wisdom in imposing that restriction. Let us correct our own miserable habit of doing the same thing.

Let me give just one illustration of how this questioning works. In 1 Timothy 6:3-5 Paul says, "If any man teach otherwise, and consent not to wholesome words, even the words of our Lord Jesus Christ, and to the doctrine which is according to godliness; he is proud, knowing nothing, but doting about the questions and strifes of words, whereof cometh envy, strife, railings, evil surmisings. Perverse disputings of men of corrupt minds, and destitute of the truth, supposing that gain is godliness: from such withdraw thyself."

Paul says to Timothy that if such a man comes to him and consents not to wholesome words, *even the words of our Lord Jesus Christ,* he is to "withdraw" from him. But instead of withdrawing from such a man, the procedure today is to make him a member of an ecumenical evangelistic campaign. He is sometimes made the treasurer or even the chairman of the effort. He is honored by being called upon to open the nightly sessions with prayer. The wisdom of God is brought into question by the leaders, and by the simple argument that they are "winning souls" the restriction is set aside.

Thanksgiving time comes and the "union meeting" is arranged. First Timothy 6:3-5 is set aside and modernists and fundamentalists join in fellowship. It is the same old temptation Satan used on Eve and Adam so long ago. Why doesn't Satan get a new temptation, you ask? Why should he when his old one works so well!

Now this method of temptation is true the world over. In 2 Corinthians 11:3,4 and 13-15 Paul says, "But I fear, lest by any means, as the serpent beguiled Eve through his subtilty, so your minds should be corrupted from the simplicity that is in Christ. For if he that cometh preacheth another Jesus, whom we have not preached, or if ye receive another spirit, which ye have not received, or another gospel, which ye have not accepted, ye might well bear with him.

"For such are false apostles, deceitful workers, transforming themselves into the apostles of Christ. And no marvel; for Satan himself is transformed into an angel of light. Therefore it is no great thing if his ministers also be transformed as the ministers of righteousness; whose end shall be according to their works."

A Counterfeit Jesus

What is Paul saying? Paul says Satan has ministers who are *ministers of righteousness,* but his ministers preach *another* gospel, *another* spirit and *another* Jesus. The modernists do preach Jesus, but it is "Another Jesus." It is a counterfeit Jesus. No counterfeiter would ever be foolish enough to take a piece of wrapping paper, print $5 on it, and expect to cash it in a bank for five good American dollars. He will spend weeks and months, even years, in producing the best plates that he hopes will defy detection. His counterfeit must be just as close as he can get it to the real thing *without being the real thing*.

That is what the Word of God says Satan is doing in this age. He is seeking to bring about the best possible conditions *apart from God*. He is trying to produce, in various realms, things that look like the genuine. It takes a real Bible-taught believer who knows what his Bible says to know the difference between the counterfeit of Satan and the genuine thing that God is offering.

Another Jesus. These "ministers" go into their pulpits and preach Jesus—"Jesus the Master," "Jesus the Example," "Jesus the lowly Nazarene," "Jesus the piteous and compassionate One." But the Jesus they preach doesn't bleed. The Jesus whom Satan's ministers are preaching in pulpits and seminaries over the world is a Jesus of lovely character and exemplary conduct. They say He is the best man who ever lived, but their own logic denies that very statement. Jesus Christ said He was God. He said that He was the Son of God. He said that He and the Father were one, that He was in existence before Abraham was. Now if Jesus Christ is not all He claimed to be, then He is not a "good man," for good men are not liars. Jesus Christ said He was God and that He came down from Heaven to die for men's sins. He said that after they killed Him, He would rise from the dead, go back to Heaven, and send the Holy Spirit. *And He did.* If He was not God incarnate, then He lied. Where I came from, liars are not good men. Jesus Christ must be the *God-Man* or He cannot possibly be a *good man*. But that is the Jesus that these ministers of Satan, described in 2 Corinthians 11, preach every Sunday—a Jesus of lovely character, but no saving blood. They say men are saved by loving like He loved and living like He lived. They forget that we are dead in trespasses and sins, and dead men cannot copy anybody.

Not only another Jesus, but another gospel. Mark those words: *another* gospel. Not the gospel that you heard from me, Paul said, but *another* gospel, the gospel that says that you are saved by works, the gospel that says we are all sons of a universal Father, and all we need as disobedient children is to come to the One who is already our Father and say, "Father, please forgive us. We will be better from now on." God then forgives and accepts us into full membership in the royal family. Counterfeit. It looks almost like the real thing, but it stops short of Calvary.

And another spirit—the spirit of love, the spirit of brotherhood, the spirit of sacrifice, the spirit of altruism, but not the Holy Spirit. So he deceives the whole world.

This deception is true in the political world. He is trying his best to get a political system and an economic system which will operate apart from God. He has already succeeded in taking God out of our schools, and Chief Justice Earl Warren has ruled that the motto "In God We Trust" cannot be inscribed on the walls of the justice chamber in Washington.

Take it from the standpoint of communism. It is a striking thing that the very basic thing that communism claims to be driving for and offers its followers is the same thing that God the Father has already offered to the peoples of this world.

Deniers of Deity

I will never forget how startled I was when, as a young preacher, in Roulette, Pennsylvania, in 1912, I heard Eugene V. Debs, the then Socialist candidate for president, speak. He said when socialism is in power, men will live under their own vine and fig tree and in their own homes and nobody will molest or destroy. When socialism is in effect, they will beat their swords into plowshares and their spears into pruning hooks. In the same address he said, "There are three great men—Herr Bebel, Karl Marx, and Jesus Christ," and he gave them in that order. I went to him and said, "Mr. Debs, was it accidental that you started on your big finger and went down to your little

finger when you named these three men?" He replied,
"No, sir. Of these three men, Jesus Christ is the least
important."

I went home puzzled. I said, "Lord, didn't I read those
same words in your Holy Bible—in Ezekiel, Isaiah, Jeremiah, Zephaniah, and other places? Did I not read there
about swords and plowshares, vines and fig trees?" I turned
and read them again. In my bewilderment I said, "Lord,
what is this all about? Are these men right? If they are
after the same thing you have said you are going to give
this earth, then I ought to be one with them instead of
fighting them. I must know, Lord." Then I went to my
Book again, and I discovered the truth. The socialists and
now the Communists, insist that these utopian conditions
are to be brought to pass on the earth by the election of
presidents and congressmen, who through a political system, will see to it that every man gets his fair share of
production and each will have his own vine and fig tree.
It is going to be done by the inauguration of a political
principle implemented by men elected to public office. My
Book said, however, that the *Lord God is going to do it by
the enthronement of His own Son!* In the day of His reign,
and not until then, will every man live under his own
vine and fig tree and none shall molest.

God says He is offering us a world of peace and plenty
and brotherhood. But it is wrapped up in Jesus Christ.
We will have it in Christ, or we will not have it at all. The
political economies of the day, and not only communism,
but all of our political schemes and systems and philosophies, in essence, say the same thing. "We want what is
in the package, but we will not take the Christ along with
it, count us out."

We could go on through the realms of the world—the
world of religion, the world of finance, the world of education—everything—and find that Satan's world system is
drilling right down to the grass roots with a deceptive
philosophy in every realm. He seems to be getting along
fairly well with it. But one of these days, thank God,
Satan's world system will end. Just as Saul's kingdom
came to an end, and David came out of the caves and the

forest of rejection and took his rightful place, so Satan, the usurper and the deceiver, will be set aside and cast into the pit. You read it in the nineteenth chapter of Revelation. Then King Jesus will come riding. In Philippians 2 we are told that He Who was equal with God and thought it not robbery to be so, laid aside the form of His deity (not His deity, but the form of it), took upon Himself the form of man, humbled Himself and became obedient unto death, even the death of the cross—seven specific steps of humbling from up there in His equality and likeness of God down to the very gates of Hell, bearing your sins and mine. The instant that Paul said that, He started on the upward bound. Because He came down and down and down, *therefore*, God has lifted Him up and up and up. There are seven more steps on the way back. And when He gets to the top of the ladder of exaltation, we read, " . . . God also hath highly exalted Him, and given Him a name which is above every name: That at the name of Jesus every knee should bow. . . . And that every tongue should confess that Jesus Christ is Lord. . . ."

God will not keep silent forever. One of these days He is coming back, and God will bring before His holy Son every blasphemer, every deity-denier, every false prophet that has stood in the churches of Jesus Christ and led the people down the broad way to an endless doom. They will be there. Don't ever think that God sent His Son into this world to bear the shame, the calumny, the disgrace and the manhandling, the bruising and the beating, the lying, the spittle, the beard-plucking, and all the rest that His Son endured without decreeing that this same Son will be exonerated and His every claim vindicated.

The deniers of His deity will stand before the blaze of His glory and God will tear their jaws open and break their knees and they will bow before that throne and say, "Thou art the Lord." They will say it, but it will not save them. Their confession is too late for that. They will turn away from that throne-sitter, having acknowledged that everything He said about Himself and everything His Father said about Him is true. They will turn away from it to enter the wide, swinging, brazen doors of the penitentiary of the universe and the lake of fire where Satan himself has already been cast, waiting for the coming of those whom he duped and damned by his system of deceit.

What an awful end to Satan's world system and those who cooperated with him in its development!

The Call to Battle

David Martyn Lloyd-Jones (1898-1981) was born in Wales and was taken to London in 1914. There he trained for a medical career and was associated with the famous Dr. Thomas Horder in Harley Street. He abandoned medicine for the gospel ministry, and from 1927 to 1938 he served the Presbyterian Church at Sandfields, Aberavon, Wales. In 1938, he became associate minister with Dr. G. Campbell Morgan at the Westminster Chapel, London; and in 1943, when Morgan retired, Lloyd-Jones succeeded him. His expositions of the Scriptures attracted great crowds wherever he preached. He retired in 1968 to devote his time to writing and limited itinerant ministry. Calvinistic in doctrine, he emphasized the "plight of man and the power of God to save."

This message is reprinted from *The Christian Soldier (Eph. 6:10-20)*, published by Baker Book House and used by permission of the family and the publishers.

David Martyn Lloyd-Jones

4

THE CALL TO BATTLE

Finally, my brethren, be strong in the Lord, and in the power of His might. Put on the whole armor of God, that ye may be able to stand against the wiles of the devil (Ephesians 6:10-11).

THERE IS NOTHING that is more urgently important for all who claim the name of Christian, than to grasp and to understand the teaching of this particular section of Scripture. I say those "who claim the name of Christian," because the Apostle's words are obviously addressed to Christian people, and to Christian people only. They have no message for those who are not Christians; indeed nobody else can understand them. The world today ridicules this kind of statement. It does not believe in a spiritual realm at all. It is even doubtful about the being of God; it has no faith in the Lord Jesus Christ; still less, therefore, does it believe that there are "principalities and powers, the rulers of the darkness of this world, spiritual wickedness even in high (or in heavenly) places." Such words are meaningless to the world; it has no appreciation of their value and importance.

But to the Christian the statement is not only full of significance, it is also full of help and of real encouragement; and, let me repeat, there is surely no theme more urgently important to all Christians at the present time than just this. I refer, of course, to the whole state of life, the whole state of the world, and to all the difficulty of living, and especially living the Christian life in these confused times in which we find ourselves.

Not that I suggest that life has ever been easy in this world for the Christian. It was not so for the early Christians. And today, in some respects, the problem is more acute and more urgent, perhaps, than it has ever been.

There was a time, until comparatively recently, when at least a man's home was more or less shut off from the world; but now the world comes into the home in many different ways, not only with the newspapers but with the television and the wireless and other media. Thus the fight of faith becomes particularly difficult and strenuous for the Christian at such a time; and in addition to all this there is the general strain of the times and anxiety of the hour.

Called to Battle

It is because of such considerations that we spent so much time in a previous volume in analyzing and considering Paul's great statement. We were occupied there in dealing with "the wiles of the devil," trying to understand what it means when it says that we are "wrestling, not against flesh and blood" (in ourselves, or in any other people), but against these spiritual powers and potentates, these principalities, these unseen hordes of wickedness that are at the back of evil, controlling the minds of evil men and all their activities, and that are set against us in order to try to defeat us, to spoil our Christian lives and bring the whole of the Gospel into disrepute. Such occupation on our part was essential. A man who does not understand the nature of the problem he is confronting is a man who is already doomed to failure. Christian people are like first-year college students—they think at first that every subject is quite simple, there is no difficulty. Well, we know what is likely to happen to such when they face an examination! The first thing you have to do is to understand the nature and the character of your problem. So we have to realize that we are called, in the Christian life, to a battle, not to a life of ease; to a battle, to a warfare, to a wrestle, to a struggle. Already we have looked in detail at the varied, almost endless ways in which the devil in his wiliness and subtlety tries to trap and to ensnare, to confuse and to confound the Christian. For the Christian to be forewarned as to the character and strategy of the enemy is absolutely essential, for to be forewarned is to be forearmed, and that in itself is half the battle.

But let us remember that it is only half the battle. Were we to leave it at that we should all undoubtedly be depressed. We would say, "Life is sufficient enough as it is without your dragging out all these things. You show us that the problem is such that no man is adequate to deal with it. You emphasize that we wrestle against terrible powers and principalities. Who is sufficient for these things? Who can stand against such massed hordes of evil, with all their subtlety and malign power?" To consider the problem in isolation, even though absolutely essential, could lead to no result except that we should all feel depressed and completely and entirely hopeless. But, thank God, the Gospel is always realistic. It never hides any of the truth, it never gives a false impression. It is not a true Gospel that gives us the impression that the Christian life is easy, and that there are no problems to be faced. That is not the New Testament teaching. The New Testament is most alarming at first, indeed terrifying, as it shows us the problems by which we are confronted. But follow it—go on! It does not stop halfway, it goes on to this addition, this second half; and here it shows us the way in which, though that is the truth concerning the battle, we can be enabled to wage it, and not only to wage it, but to triumph in it. It shows us that we are meant to be "more than conquerors."

Confronting the Problem

So the Apostle goes on to show us this second half; and he does so in his own characteristic manner. He even puts this before he states the problem. He says, "Be strong in the Lord, and in the power of His might. Put on the whole armor of God, that" (in order that)—then he introduces the problem. Here, I say, is something for which we should thank God always. Here, and here alone, we are told that, despite all that is against us, whether in realms above or in the world in which we live with all its strains and stresses, as Christian people we can be enabled to triumph, to rejoice in the midst of it all, and to know that victory is assured. That is the matter to which we now turn.

What is offered us as we find ourselves, as Christian people, facing all this—this wrestling, this struggling, this combat? You notice that there are just two things. First, "Be strong in the Lord, and in the power of His might"; second, "Take unto you the whole armor of God."

As we come to look at these two things there are some preliminary comments that I have to make. The first is that both these are necessary. We are not to take one without the other. The Apostle says both, and we have to do both. We shall have occasion to repeat that constantly as we go along. But notice the order in which he puts them. He does not tell you to put on the armor first, and then to be strong in the Lord. No, it is the other way around: "Be strong in the Lord, and in the power of His might"; then, "Take unto you the whole armor of God." There is a very real significance in the order. I will have occasion later to show its significance and the importance of following it as a practical issue.

There is clearly a relationship between the two factors. Let me just hint at what will be developed as we proceed. It is this: that so often people take just one or the other of these factors and therefore make shipwreck of the faith. There are some who say, "All you need to do is to hand it over to the Lord and rely on His strength." They never say anything about "the whole armor of God"—that is left out completely. There are others who put their whole emphasis on the putting on of the armor of God, as if they could wield it themselves. They forget their absolute dependence upon the power of the Lord, and His might and His strength. We see then that there are several interesting matters in the mere presentation of the two things which are essential to a triumphant living of the Christian life.

The Source of Our Strength

Let us start, then, with the first—"Be strong in the Lord, and in the power of His might." Here is a great order issued by this mighty captain, the Apostle Paul—an order for the day. Here is a word sent out to the Christian army gathered together, with the enemy there in position facing it. Here is the word that comes from this great leader who himself had had long experience in warfare personally, and who, as he reminds us so often, had the care of all the churches upon him, and had seen at first hand the machinations of the evil one against God's people. Here then is a great order for the day—"Be strong in the Lord, and in the power of His might." Hold on to this, do not forget it. In the heat and the thick of the battle later on in the day, whatever happens, never forget, never lose sight of, this great guiding and controlling principle.

But what does it mean, and how are we to do it? It is a resounding phrase. To read it, to repeat it, is not enough. We like singing the words of the hymn, "Put on the Gospel Armor." But what does it mean in practice? Let us investigate the matter. Christianity is not a form of psychology. You do not just walk along the road saying, "Be strong in the Lord, and in the power of His might," using it as some kind of incantation, or auto-suggestion, repeating the phrases to yourself. That is not Christianity at all! It is true of the cults, of course; it is the psychological method. You repeat the phrases such as, "Every day, and in every way, I am getting better and better." You persuade yourself, and you think less and less about your health, and you therefore begin to feel better. Up to a point it works, but only up to a point.

But in any case, as I say, it is not the Christian message. So often we are in danger of abusing the Scriptures in this way. We use them as mere phrases in that manner, or lightheartedly we sing our hymns, and we feel better for the time being. But the question is, How do we stand up to temptations when we are in the street outside, and what are we like at home? When you turn Scripture into a drug, into something which gives you a temporary relief without your knowing why or how, the effect does not last. It gives a temporary feeling of exhilaration, but fails you when you are in the struggle and in the heat of the battle.

What, then, is the true application of the Apostle's precept? The first thing to realize is the need to be strong because of the power of the enemy. Never underestimate that power. The Bible always calls us to face the enemy and to realize that he is, as Peter says, "as a roaring lion,

seeking whom he may devour." We are told that the archangel Michael dared not speak lightly or loosely to him,
and when he debated with him concerning the body of
Moses he did not bring any "railing accusation" against
him. All the archangel ventured to say was, "The Lord
rebuke thee" (Jude 9). The enemy is terribly powerful and
full of wiles and of subtlety and of guile; he can even
"transform himself into an angel of light" (2 Cor. 11:14).

Another reason, and a very practical one from the human side, is that if you are to be able to stand, and
withstand in the evil day, you need this strength. "The
evil day!" Though the Christian life in one sense is always
the same kind of life, there are variations; there are evil
days, some days are worse than others; they are excep-
tionally bad. In general at the present time we are living
in a very "evil" day. It is evil in every respect. I am not
only thinking of international tensions; it is an evil day
because evil and sin are so powerfully organized, so deeply entrenched; it is an evil day because of the confusion in
the Church herself which sometimes seems to deny not
only the whole of the Gospel but even belief in the being
of God Himself. It is not easy to be a Christian at a time
like this when you have men in positions of high authority in the Church talking about "meeting atheists in heav-
en!" Christians are being confused by these things,
particularly, perhaps, young Christians. The devil is un-
usually busy and active, creating this uncertainty about
the essentials of the faith and producing this utter confusion—"What is the Gospel? What is not the Gospel?" Undoubtedly we live in a very evil day; and if we are to
withstand at such a time as this, there is only one way;
and it is the way the Apostle teaches us here. We need
this power, and the whole armor of God; and then we
shall be able to stand. Thank God that this is so. Though
the confusion is terrible, those who believe the truth still
can stand. Do not be disheartened, do not be discouraged,
do not be misled, do not be put off. You may be standing
alone, perhaps, but you can still be enabled to stand though
the days are so cruelly evil and vile and foul.

But there are other reasons which should encourage

us all to seek this strength and this power. Why should I be "strong in the Lord, and in the power of His might"? I answer: I wish to be strong in order to avoid personal failure; for I know that, when I do fail and fall into sin, I become miserable and unhappy. This is true of all Christians. So, to save yourself from the misery that is the inevitable consequence of any failure in the Christian life, "be strong in the Lord, and in the power of His might."

But I will give you a much higher reason than the fear of personal failure. "Be strong" because you are who you are, because you are what you are. We are individuals in this matter of salvation but we are not isolated units. We are members severally of the body of Christ; we belong to Him, to God's family. Remember this always, that the Lord Jesus Christ is "not ashamed to call us brethren" (Heb. 2:11). Remember also that "God is not ashamed to be called (your) God" (Heb. 11:16). The Name of God is upon us, the Name of Christ is upon us. Why should I be strong? Well, for His sake even more than for my own sake. In a sense this is an alarming thought, and yet it is one of the most glorious truths we can ever realize about ourselves—that the reputation, as it were, of Almighty God, Father, Son and Holy Spirit, is in our hands, and any failure in us brings the great and holy Name into disrepute. We are not isolated individuals, we are one in this great and mighty army.

The world knows how to respond to these appeals, does it not? Nelson knew exactly what he was doing on the morning of Trafalgar: "England expects that every man this day will do his duty." Certainly! The name of the country! Multiply that by infinity and see that you and I have no right to be weak because our failure not only involves ourselves. The whole family in heaven and in earth is involved with us. We are representatives.

It is not only that we may live a happier life that I am calling attention to this text. Let us abandon this purely subjective approach, let us learn to look at things from the standpoint of the Church of the living God, this great army with banners; let us think of Him who is the Captain and Leader of our salvation. And let us remember that we belong to Him, and that anything that happens to us inevitably involves Him also.

So, finally, I put the matter thus. There is no better way of giving a proof of the truth of the Gospel than that we should "be strong in the Lord, and in the power of His might," than that we should triumph and prevail. To live aright is difficult, and when we see someone who is succeeding, someone who can stand against the enticements and the insinuations of evil, someone who is not carried away off his feet by the popular thing, someone who stands steadfastly for truth and for everything that is worthy, we are greatly encouraged. It undoubtedly has a great effect on those who are looking on.

We are all being watched at the present time. The world is most unhappy, men and women do not know what to do, they do not know where to turn. When they see someone who seems to be calm and steadfast, someone who is not utterly bewildered at a time like this, someone who seems to have an insight into it all, and who can see beyond it all, they look and they say, "What is this? What is that person's secret?" And so you become an evangelist by just standing and being "strong in the Lord, and in the power of His might." You are not carried away by the flood, you do not do things because everyone else is doing them, you have principles of your own, and you are ready to stand for them and to suffer for them. That has often been the means, under God's blessing, of awakening others and convicting them of sin, and causing them to begin to inquire after God.

In our daily lives, whatever our earthly calling, we all live in some kind of circle; we are surrounded by people who are blinded by the devil and carried along in evil ways by him at his will (2 Tim. 2:26). You never know when the mere fact that you are just "standing" may arrest attention and open a door of opportunity for the saving Gospel of our Lord Jesus Christ.

There, then, are some reasons and preliminary considerations why we must be strong in the Lord, and in the power of His might.

The Reality of Our Weakness

In the second place, we have to realize our own weakness and our need of help. That is the presupposition behind what the Apostle is saying here. He is not only concerned about this because of the power of the enemy, he is equally concerned because of our own weakness, our own lack of strength; and, again, the best way of realizing this impotency is to understand something of the power of the enemy. There is ample teaching in the Bible to bring you to that knowledge. Go back to the very beginning of the Bible. You find there is a man called Adam who was sinless and perfect. But he is confronted by the devil, and the manifestation of "the wiles of the devil." Though Adam was perfect, and had lived a life of fellowship and communion with God, he fell; and he fell so easily! The subtlety of the enemy with his insinuation that God was against man, that God was unfair to man, was too much for Adam and he fell. When the devil launches his attack, what is man, even perfect man made in the image of God? Adam fell. And if Adam in that perfect state fell, who are we to stand?

But let us go further. Look at the Old Testament saints, all of them, the patriarchs, the godly kings, and the prophets. They all fell, not one of them could stand up to the devil. He is "the strong man armed, that keepeth his goods at peace." All men have failed, they have all "sinned and come short of the glory of God"; they have succumbed to "the wiles of the devil."

This has also been the universal testimony of all Christian saints, the greatest saints of the centuries. It is one of the hallmarks of the true saint, that he never gives the impression that the Christian life is an easy one—never! The man who gives the impression that it is easy has confused something else with Christianity; he has a short-cut which he imagines brings him to a place where everything is quite simple. But that is never the Christian way. The greatest saints have always testified to the fierceness of the battle, to their own weakness, to their own ability. They have mourned over this. Let us then pay heed to what this great "cloud of witnesses" is saying to us today.

But let me commend to you also the study of your own experience. If you feel that you are a very strong Christian, let me ask you why you have failed so much and why you still fail? What happens to your resolutions and resolves? Why do you so often find yourself in the place of repentance? Why are you sometimes attacked with feelings of utter hopelessness and almost despair? To what is it due? It is all due to the plain fact of our weakness; it is because we are insufficient and fallible.

But we must face this honestly. It is not enough just to say in general, "Yes, I know the enemy is very strong, as you say, and I am weak." We have to persuade ourselves of our weakness. This is half the battle. We need to know that we are ill; in other words we need to indulge in a great deal of self-examination. That is why people pay such slight heed to our text; that is why we know so little about what it is to stand, and to be strong in the Lord, and in the power of His might; we have never realized our own need. "They that are whole have no need of a physician." That was the chief trouble with the Pharisees. They thought they were right with God; they did not go to the doctor; there was nothing wrong with them. We do not go to the doctor as long as we feel that all is well; we have to realize that we are "sick." But that means examination, self-examination. In that way only shall we discover the elements of weakness that are in us inherently, and that render us incapable of fighting the battle against sin and Satan.

Another thing we have to realize is that mere principles of morality are not sufficient for us. The world has always been interested in what it calls "the good life." Philosophers have always been interested in the subject; they have written about it, talked about it, and argued about it. But the trouble has been that they were never able to practice it. Principles of morality are good as far as they go, but they are not enough; you can read books on ethics and can wax eloquent on these matters, but it is a very different thing to put them into practice. "To will is present with me, but how to perform that which is good I know not," said the Apostle (Rom. 7:18). I see that a certain thing is right, but the problem is, "How am I to do it?" And it is when you really face the problem that you begin to realize the extent of your weakness.

Furthermore, human will-power alone is not enough. Will-power is excellent and we should always be using it; but it is not enough. A desire to live a good life is not enough. Obviously we should all have that desire, but it will not guarantee success. So let me put it thus: Hold on to your principles of morality and ethics, use your will-power to the limit, pay great heed to every noble, uplifting desire that is in you; but realize that these things alone are not enough, that they will never bring you to the desired place. We have to realize that all our best is totally inadequate, that a spiritual battle must be fought in a spiritual manner. This has been put well in a hymn by Isaac Watts:

> From Thee, the overflowing spring,
> Our souls shall drink a fresh supply,
> While such as trust their native strength
> *Shall melt away, and droop, and die.*

That is true! Remember also the words of another hymn:

> The arm of flesh will fail you,
> *You dare not trust your own.*

Here we have the very beginning of an understanding of this whole matter. The problem is not just a problem in moral living. That is the limit of the State's concern with our persons. The State knows nothing about the spiritual background, for it knows nothing about the devil and "the principalities and powers." And that is why it continues to believe that education can really solve the problem and reform persons. That is why it evokes the aid of psychotherapy and various other expedients in prisons. But the more it does so the more the problem seems to increase. It is all because men do not realize the spiritual character of the problem.

You and I have to realize that the living of the Christian life does not follow automatically upon conversion. Many a man, having come into the Christian life through regeneration, through a true experience, has then tried to live the Christian life in the old terms. He thinks that he needs the act of God in Christ to save him, but he seems to leave it at that. He feels that henceforward he is going to live the Christian life by his own power; he has a new understanding so now he is going to live this life. But it cannot be done! This is the road along which people "melt away, and droop, and die," because they are trusting to nothing but their "native strength." On the contrary, this is a battle that has to be fought in a spiritual manner and with spiritual understanding.

The Meaning of His Might

That leads us to the third general principle. Having realized that I am to be strong and that in and of myself I am essentially weak, because I am still in the flesh and that it is still true that "the flesh lusteth against the Spirit, and the Spirit against the flesh, and these are contrary one to the other"—realizing that all that is still true of me, and that I am here in this warfare, and up against this terrible power, what is the next thing? It is to realize that the Lord is strong, that He is mighty, and, as the Old Testament reminds us, that "The name of the Lord is a strong tower." His very Name is strong. The Name represents Him, who He is and what He is. And the first thing, therefore, we have to realize is the greatness of His strength. That is what the Apostle is saying to the Ephesians and to us.

Listen to the words; examine them in detail. He says, "Be strong in the Lord, and in the power of His might." Do we realize its full significance? What does he mean by "the power of His might"? The basic thing, obviously, is the "might." We are directed to "the power" of His "might." The difference between power and might is that *might* means power and strength as an enduement; *might* means inherent power, something a man is given. Think of a very strong, muscular man. The "might" is that man's inherent muscular strength and power. Power means the manifestation of that might; the might is there as a potential, as something inherent, now manifesting itself, showing its efficacy, showing that it can be effectual. It means this great reserve of strength and power is actually in operation, doing something; not the enduement itself but the proof of the fact that you have the enduement.

So the Apostle uses the two terms, and it is important that we should look at both. He says, "Be strong in the Lord, and in the might of His strength"; so you start by reminding yourself of His strength. Look at Him, he says, look at His power. You have been looking at the enemy and you have seen his strength; you have looked at yourself and you are trembling in your weakness and in your ineffectiveness; well, now, he says, look at Him, "Be strong in the Lord."

To be "strong in the Lord" you must remember "the might of His power"—"the might of His strength." Express it whichever way you like, but look at Him and realize all the reserves of strength and power that are in Him. That is what these New Testament Epistles are saying almost everywhere. "In him," says the Apostle Paul to the Colossians, "dwelleth all the fullness of the Godhead bodily." It is there in Him. "In whom," he says again, "God has hid all the treasures of wisdom and of knowledge" (2:3). They are all there. They constitute this might, this tremendous inherent strength and power. To be strong in the Lord means meditating about Him and His strength. It is not just a phrase, an incantation, a formula. It means that you sit down and remind yourself of these things, and you look at Him, and you remind yourself of some of the things that are true concerning Him.

Incidentally, that we may do just this is one of the main reasons for reading Scriptures regularly, and reading the four Gospels in particular. We should not read the Scriptures merely in order that we may say that we have read our daily portion, and so have done our duty. That is no reason for reading the Scriptures. I am not attacking systematic reading; I am a great advocate of systematic reading. All I am saying is that you should be careful that the devil in his wiliness does not come in and make you content with a mere mechanical reading of the Scriptures without really looking at them, and meditating upon them without realizing what they are saying, and without drawing lessons for yourself, and praying about the exercise. It takes time to read Scripture properly. It is very easy to read a number of verses and rush off to catch your bus or train. That is not reading the Scriptures; that may be quite useless. You must stop and look and think. So go back to the Gospels and look at Him and "the power of His strength."

Where do I see His strength? I see it in His life. I see Him here in this world in the "likeness of sinful flesh." I see Him in the same world as I am in. I see that obviously He knew hunger and thirst and physical weakness and tiredness, that He knew what it was to be disappointed with people. He has gone through it all. And yet what I see, as I look at Him, is that He stands, He always stands. There is never a wavering, still less a failing or a faltering or a falling. He stood, with the world and the flesh and the devil—everything—against Him. He stood. Therefore as I look at His life I see at once One who walked through this world without deviating in any respect. He just went on steadily.

I see even more than that, I see it in all His miracles. I see it especially in the miracles in which He cast out devils. Here is One to whom they were not a problem. Here is One who can command the devils. He can exorcise them. He speaks with power and with authority and the devils have to come cringing to Him, asking Him to spare them, not to cast them into the deep that they might be destroyed. Here is a Master. They come to Him and say, "We know you are the Holy One of God." Here is the One who, when the devils are operating powerfully, with a word could drive them out. The disciples could not do that. Look at the boy at the foot of the Mount of Transfiguration. The father had brought the boy to the disciples and they had done their best. But they could not help, and the poor boy remained a victim of Satan's power. But at a word from our Lord the devil is driven out and the boy is healed and is restored to his father. There we see His power in operation, there we see something of "the power of His might." He is the master of "the principalities and powers, the rulers of the darkness of this world, the spiritual wickedness in high places" (Eph. 3:10).

But we must go still further and observe this "power of His might" as it is revealed in His own temptation. He was tried directly by the devil himself, not by some of the emissaries, not by one or the other of these principalities or powers, but by the devil himself with all his wiles. Here the devil himself takes charge of the situation because he realizes that it is the biggest problem he has ever confronted. So he came to our Lord and tempted Him forty days and forty nights in the wilderness and on other occasions; but he was utterly and entirely defeated. With the words of Scripture our Lord repels him, and the devil falls back defeated, waiting for another season. But he completely failed in spite of many efforts.

That is what we must dwell upon and consider. This is not just a detail or an incident in the life of our Lord which helps you to understand His Person. It does that, of course, and attests His Person; but now, says the Apostle: Make practical use of it. Take it up, take hold of that power yourself. There, you see, He met in single combat the devil with all his power in operation, and He easily defeated him, therefore "Be strong in the Lord, and in the power of His might." The power was always and already in Him; and when the devil comes He just shows it, He just lets a little of it out, as it were, and the devil is immediately repulsed. Lay hold of that, says the Apostle.

James, in exactly the same way, and grasping this point says, "Resist the devil and he will flee from you" (4:7). That is the way it works out. But it does not work out until you and I are quite certain about Christ's power, and really do know something of "the power of His might," the inherent power that is in Him. "In Him dwelleth all the fullness of the Godhead bodily." He is both God and Man. He cannot fail. He did not fail.

Finally, of course, the Lord proves and demonstrates His power on the Cross and in the Resurrection. The Cross seems to be the day of the power of evil. The powers of evil thought that to be the case, as also did the devil and all his hosts. The world, too, had similar thoughts. They reviled Him, they laughed at Him, they jeered, "Thou savest others, come down, save Thyself." They thought that He could not do so, and that the devil had defeated Him! But what was happening there was that "He was taking these principalities and powers" (says Paul in Col. 2:15) "and putting them to an open shame, triumphing over them in it" (by it). That is, He was triumphing over them when they thought that they had defeated Him. "Now is the judgment of this world," He says beforehand, looking at the Cross. "Now is the prince of this world cast out (cast forth)" (John 12:31). So look at the Cross and meditate upon it. This is the supreme paradox: He appears to be dying in weakness, but do you see the inherent strength there, do you see this might of His, do you see the power of the Godhead there, turning even that into the vanquishing of the devil and the setting of His people free—a glorious victorious triumph? Look at it and see just that!

Then go on and look at the Resurrection. He "bursts asunder the bands of death," triumphs over the last enemy, and the ultimate effects of sin and evil. He is master completely over all these powers that are set against us, He defeats them all. He rises, He ascends into heaven, "leading captivity captive." He is the conqueror over everything that is set against us.

This is not some psychological formula that you and I can apply. But it all comes back to this—to know Him! You will never know power in your life until you know Him. So we must get to know Him. We shall find when we consider the various portions of the "armor" that they are nearly all directed to that end, to know Him, to know about Him and the truth concerning Him. We start with that here—"in the Lord, and in the power of His might."

Do we realize something of this? Do we know anything about it? Forget yourself for the time being. Look at Him and realize the truth about Him. Then realize that His power is available for you. That is the key to it all. So we must look at Him objectively as He is portrayed to us, as He reveals Himself to us. Then we must realize that we belong to One who is "the Lord" and that "all the fullness of the Godhead" is in Him, that there is invincible might and power in Him, and that it is a might and power that not only remains *potential*, but also becomes *actual*. It shows itself, it manifests itself on our behalf and also in us. So here we begin to look at this saving word that enables us even in this evil day to stand, to withstand, to be strong, to fight the battle of the Lord, and to bring honor and glory to His great and holy Name.

The Christian Conflict

George Campbell Morgan (1863-1945) was the son of a British Baptist preacher and preached his first sermon when he was 13 years old. He had no formal training for the ministry, but his tireless devotion to the study of the Bible helped him to become one of the leading Bible teachers of his day. Rejected by the Methodists, he was ordained into the Congregational ministry. He was associated with Dwight L. Moody in the Northfield Bible conferences and as an itinerant Bible teacher. He is best known as the pastor of Westminster Chapel, London (1904-17 and 1933-45). During his second term there, he had Dr. D. Martyn Lloyd-Jones as his associate.

He published more than 60 books and booklets, and his sermons are found in *The Westminster Pulpit* (Pickering and Inglis Ltd., London). This sermon was given at Bristol Keswick and is found in *Keswick's Triumphant Voice*, edited by Herbert F. Stevenson, published by Zondervan and used by their permission.

George Campbell Morgan

5

THE CHRISTIAN CONFLICT

IN EPHESIANS 6:13 YOU WILL FIND these words, "Having done all, to stand." The reading of just these words may seem very much like the wresting of a text from its context. Beloved, I have no such intention. I take for granted your familiarity with the context, and shall make, more than once, reference thereto. I do desire, however, that the tone and suggestiveness of this particular phrase shall arrest our attention, and shall indicate the line of our meditation.

An Assured Victory

"Having done all, to stand." Paul's words have in them the ring of *an assured victory*. They suggest nothing of doubt, nothing of despondency. There is nothing hypothetical, to the thinking of this man, as to the matter of the issue of a certain fight which he is describing. I think perhaps I might say that this little phrase, in some sense, might be omitted; and the great argument of the paragraph in which it stands would not be interfered with by the omission. It is a sort of shout of triumph in the midst of a description. It is a phrase that gives utterance to the writer's own sure and absolute confidence in the presence of conflict: "Having done all, to stand."

While it is true that the phrase taken alone is suggestive of victory, that becomes far more evident when it is considered, as it must finally be considered, in its contextual relationship. You notice that it is part of a paragraph in the letter commencing in our Bibles at verse 10 with these words: "Finally, be strong in the Lord, and in the strength of His might"; and in the course of the passage beginning there, and ending, shall we say, at verse 18, the conflict is evidently in view: the contestants are clearly seen; the enemies are presented before us—"principalities, powers, the world-rulers of this darkness, spiritual hosts of wickedness in holy places"; and the equipment of the soldier-saint is described with remarkable accuracy, and is seen to be a perfect equipment. You remember the words—we are not going to stay to dwell upon them—the loins girt with truth; the breastplate of righteousness; feet shod with the preparation (or, the *readiness*) of the Gospel of peace; the shield of faith, the helmet of salvation; and one weapon only—the sword of the Spirit, which is the Word of God; and a clearly defined condition, "With all prayer and supplication praying at all seasons in the Spirit."

An Actual Conflict

The passage brings before us, with no less clarity, the *actuality of conflict.* If I take certain phrases out from it, it will be sufficient to show how true that is. The apostle's word, "We wrestle not against flesh and blood." We wrestle—it is a word that indicates actual, positive, definite conflict. And then the necessaries for the waging of the warfare. Notice carefully the two things: "Take up the whole armor of God," but, prior to that, "Put on the whole armor of God." Put on, and take up. Put on the panoply of God; take up the panoply of God. Perfect equipment: and yet not merely equipment for military display, but for actual warfare. Take it up.

And, once again, take out these words from the whole passage: we are told that we are to s*tand* in the evil day; that we are to *withstand*; and finally, having done all, to *stand*. The foes, I repeat, are seen; the equipment is described; the conflict is recognized. And in the midst of it all comes out this little phrase, "Having done all, to stand." There is no quaver in the voice, there is no suggestion in the mind of this man that there can be defeat. Yes, you say, he is referring to some ultimate and final fight, as indicated by his words, "Finally, my brethren. . . ." He does not refer to the last thing in Christian experience, but to the last thing in his letter. He was saying, What I have written already makes necessary the last thing: "finally, be strong in the Lord, and in the strength of His might." And he shows that the life he has been describing means conflict.

What, then, is the thought before us? The question is constantly being asked, especially by young Christians, "Is the victorious life possible, after all?" I am not proposing to deal with the subject as it affects the inner life of the believer. I want to speak of the conflict with the forces that are without; and in the presence of these, I say, the question is perpetually being asked, "Is a victorious Christian life possible?" We all know the conflict; at least, we do if we are Christian people. We are all more or less familiar with the forces that are against us in our Christian life—forces without, but nonetheless real and terrible. Here is the question in the minds of many: "Is it possible so to fight as always, having done all, to stand— to stand against the foe?"

Yes, to withstand, assuredly. But can I add to the stand and to the withstand, the apostle's word, "Having done all, to stand"? Now I want, first of all, to go a little away from this paragraph, and to say this while I address myself, as far as I am able, to those who are face to face with that question. A great many of you settled it long ago. By the infinite grace and power of God, you entered into experience of the victorious life. That is not a life without *conflict*, but it is a life without *defeat*. I ask your prayer and your intercession, that someone who is today facing this one problem may be helped to find an answer.

And now, first, this is what I want to say: No one can answer this question for you finally. You will have to discover the final answer in your own experience, by making the great adventure. That may seem to cut away the ground from under my own feet; and you may be inclined to say to me, Why speak to us at all? My brethren, the theory taught even in the Word, and the testimony borne by the saints, recorded in the Word, and through the centuries, these things are not enough to bring to you ultimate and final demonstration in answer to your inquiry as to whether you can live the victorious Christian life. There is only one way for you to find out—discover the teaching of the Word, and obey it; find out for yourself.

Not for *demonstration* is testimony borne, but for *inspiration*; to lead each one of us, for ourselves, to make the great adventure. I am inclined to think that a great many of you do not agree with that statement. I believe that here is the place where so many linger and wait, when they ought to enter into definite blessing. Sometimes I almost wish that, apart from the writings of the Word, no lives of the saints had ever been written. I say *sometimes*, not often; for I love them. A young man came to me a little while ago and said, "I mean to give the whole thing up in despair." "Why?" I asked. He made this very remarkable answer: "I have just been reading the life of Fletcher of Madeley; and it is quite hopeless, I can never know what he knew."

Now the trouble is that we read the lives of the saints, and seek to enter into the experience they describe; but God's will is that we should enter into our own experience, in fellowship with Him. There are a thousand ways of entrance into the life of victory, and a thousand varieties of experience within it; and so when I turn back to the theory or to the testimony, I only turn back in order that by it we may be inspired to make the great adventure for ourselves, and discover whether or not this thing is so. A young man has a Bible because his father gave it to him. Half the men who have lost their Bibles are those who have tried to take it as a gift from their fathers. Let that not be misunderstood. I shall thank God through time and eternity for a father whose one book was the Bible; but I had to get it for myself. I had to give myself to it before it became mine as, thank God, it is mine today—a great treasure house, which I am beginning to find I do not know, and have not explored, but long to know more perfectly. So is it in the high matter of spiritual experience.

This is not the proper order of making a sermon, to state the application first; but it is my specific purpose. I want young men and women making this inquiry to see at first that whether or not the testimony of the saints be true, and the theory of the Word of God be correct, they have to make the great adventure.

Having said so much, I turn you back again to this

apostolic writing. And, so far from taking the passage out of the context, I want the whole epistle in order to discover what it means when it says, "Having done all, to stand." There are two lines which I will follow for a few minutes in each case. First, What is the conflict which the apostle describes, and second, what are the terms of the victory—upon what grounds? That is to say, according to his experience, according to his testimony, how is the victorious life possible?

The Conflict Described

First, then, *what is the conflict which is described in this passage?* Now in order to understand it we must have the whole letter before our mind in outline. I am not going to take the Bible and turn to passages—I have not the time; but I am taking for granted your familiarity with the outline, to refresh your memory. We will look first at the soldier-saints who are described in this letter. Then, at those foes which the apostle describes in that particular passage. And we shall see, in a moment, how between the soldier-saints described, and the foes described, there must inevitably be conflict.

Now, who are these soldier-saints? You will remember how this letter, in common with all the letters of the apostle, falls into two parts. In the first part, the great doctrine is enunciated; then all the duties resulting from the doctrine are declared. Or, to put it in another way, the truth and then the triumph; the creed and then the conduct growing out of it. The dividing line in this letter is at the commencement of the fourth chapter: "I therefore, the prisoner in the Lord, beseech you to walk worthily." Of what? Of the vocation, the calling. That little phrase, "the calling" of the saints, takes us back to everything preceding. In the first three chapters you find the apostle dealing with the great mystery and glory of the Church of Christ. In chapter one—we are taking the divisions roughly; it is not quite accurate, but will suffice—he deals with the tremendous subject of predestination, God's original purpose in the Church. In chapter two, he shows the edification of the Church coming out into visibility in human history. In chapter three, he gathers up the teaching concerning the Church's vocation.

My brethren, we must get hold of this. We shall never understand what the apostle teaches at this point. He shows, first, that *the child of God, or soldier-saint, is one who shares the mystic and mighty life of the Christ Himself*: that is the fundamental position. I am inclined to say that there is very little of the real conflict until a man is born again. There may be moments in the life of the unregenerate man—indeed, I believe there are such moments—when he sees a gleam of the beauty of holiness, and sighs after it. But there is no conflict; he turns back to the beggarly elements of the world, gives himself up again to things base, low, and mean. But directly the Christ-life is in the soul by the inspiration of the Spirit, in that moment there is the consciousness of conflict.

I do not want to dwell upon the conflict now; more of that in a moment. Face this fact, that the first thing taught in this letter is that the Christian shares the life of Christ; so that whatever may be said concerning holiness, concerning the deepening of spiritual life, concerning stages of advancement in blessing, the whole thing has to do with those who already share the Christ-life. We begin there. Paul would never have written to the men of Ephesus, other than the saints, as fighting against the rulers of this world and hosts of spiritual wickedness in heavenly places. He was talking to men and women who shared the life of Christ; and there we begin, for the conflict is for such.

The Terms of Victory

The second truth taught in the letter is, that *the Christian is one whose ultimate work is not in this world, but in the next*; it lies out beyond, and out of sight today. I am coming to the present responsibility that is also taught, with great clearness, in the letter; but if the letter means anything, it means that the Church, and all the company of saints constituting that Church, will find the final vocation beyond this life altogether. Take some of the strange, majestic and marvelous passages of this letter; take a glance at them haphazard. He says, "that in the ages to

come He might show the exceeding riches of His grace in
kindness toward us in Christ Jesus." He says, "Now"—
not immediateness, but result—"unto the principalities
and the powers in the heavenlies might be made known
through the Church the manifold wisdom of God." He
distinctly teaches, in this letter, that God has an inheritance in His people; not that we have an inheritance in
Him—which is perfectly true—but something more as-
tonishing: that God has an inheritance in His people; that
God has created in His people a medium through which,
to all ages to come and to the unfallen intelligences of the
other world, He will make known His grace, and make
known His wisdom. It is the most daring and magnificent
thing ever written about the ultimate vocation of the child
of God. It shows that in the ages to come we are still to be
the messengers of His grace; and that men will only know
the grace of God, and that angels and principalities will
only know the grace of God, and that all the ages that
transcend the possibility of our imagination will only know
the grace of God, as we tell "the old, old story of Jesus and
His love." Our perfect work begins beyond.

So the apostle is speaking to a people who, in this
world, share the mystic and mighty life of the Christ; and
who, in this world, are being prepared for a final vocation
that lies beyond. Hear me, my brethren: they are other-
worldly men and women; and in the moment in which the
Church of God is afraid of that designation, she has lost
the power to touch this world.

Our Responsibility

But he teaches something else, and it is that men and
women who share the mystic life of the Christ, and whose
ultimate vocation lies beyond the present world and age,
*have immediate, definite, positive responsibility in this
world.* If you imagine that the other-worldly outlook described for a single moment interferes with interest in,
and responsibility concerning, this world, read the second
half of this epistle carefully. "I beseech you to walk worthily of the vocation. . . ." In other words, let the light of
the heavenly flash upon the earthly; let the methods of

the higher life touch all that is lower; bring to bear upon every relationship of the present life the measurement, and the adjustment, and the conceptions of this higher and truer life. You live a secret life; it is the life of union with Jesus. You live a life of preparation for a vocation that lies ahead. But the secret life and the preparatory life are to affect the present life. And if you charge the apostle with other-worldliness, I repeat: read his letter to the close. It is more practical than preachers dare to be, very often. Husbands and wives, fathers and children, masters and servants, adjust all your relationships and live out all your lives here, in this world, in the light of the heavenly calling, and in the virtues of the Christ-life which is yours by His gift and by His grace.

I may summarize that upon which I have touched in a brief outline. The soldier-saints are men and women who share the Christ-life, the ultimate meaning of whose life is service unto the ages of the ages, but who therefore have present responsibilities—those of revealing the order, and the moment, and the power, and the breadth, and the beneficence of heavenly things, amidst all the things of this world, at home, and in business, and wherever we may be. These are the soldier-saints.

Now, mark how in this passage the apostle puts over against that the enemies. "We wrestle not against flesh and blood"—and there is a touch of disdain in the way in which he refers to flesh and blood, as though it were an easy matter in comparison with the struggle and the conflict of these soldier-saints of the Most High—"not against the flesh and blood." Just as Peter dismisses as unimportant the low things, in the scheme of redemption—"not with corruptible things, such as silver and gold, but with the precious blood of Christ"—so here, when speaking of our conflict, "not against flesh and blood." Why emphasize that? Because I want to help men find out that it is a severe and a real conflict. It is a real and a severe conflict, definite, positive, and awful; and, to the very end of the chapter, this conflict is not against flesh and blood, but against principalities and powers.

Mark the massing: against the principalities and powers. The saints, who share the life of Christ and are under His Lordship, have to fight against the principalities and powers that are in rebellion against Him. "Against the world-rulers"—now mark this carefully—"of this darkness." There is a little phrase one would like to stay with. You notice the infinite significance of it. Do you understand it? What was he referring to? To Ephesus, perchance; perhaps to a group of cities. I care not. I am content to take Ephesus—"the center of light," as men said, the home of commerce, the home of wealth; the place where commerce and religion had joined at this time, so that merchantmen were banking in the temple of Artemis. If you had gone to Ephesus as another traveler went, Pausanius of old, whose description you may have read, you would have said, "This is the center of light." But the apostle, writing to men and women in Ephesus, says, "The world-rulers of this darkness." The world never looks as though it were wrapped in darkness save to the saints who have seen the coming glory, and are living in expectation of the divine order and vocation. Once you have seen that glory, once you have had a conception of that high, holy, and ultimate service, you see all the order of the present life as a darkness; and all the world-rulers of the darkness, the spirits of evil, are against the saints.

Then the apostle masses the whole in the comprehensive word, "spiritual hosts of wickedness." I do not take it to be necessary here, brethren, to say that I believe the apostle meant exactly what he wrote: that the saint has to fight not merely against the foe within—that is not the subject here—but against spiritual antagonisms without, against the devil and all his hosts, as we sometimes have to do. Here is the real conflict: it is against this that you and I are called to wage our warfare. The conflict is between those who share Christ's life, and are preparing for eternal service in the presence of their present responsibility, on the one hand, and all the fallen spirits of the higher worlds, all the hosts of wickedness that rule and inspire and master the things of this world, on the other. Against these massed forces we have to fight: and I am one of those who growingly feel that we need to recognize the adversary, and to be conscious of the fact that our battle is not merely a battle against the weakness we find within. It need not be; for in five minutes it can all be ended. But the forces are without; and the battle with them never ends while we are here.

Now someone says, We know all this experimentally, although we have never said so before: but can we win? This man says, Yes. The conflict is real; the equipment is perfect; the fight has to be waged. Withstand, and, having done all, to stand. Upon what ground did he base that word of utter and absolute confidence?

Well now, I am inclined rather to have the story of the man without going into details at all, to illustrate what seems to me to be the law of victory in this conflict. There are three things. We are very familiar with the story of the man who wrote this letter. The three things are: (1) absolute surrender to Christ; (2) patient discipline under His training; and (3) actual and unceasing conflict. And where these things are so, and are observed, what then? Stand, withstand, fight; and, having done all, stand.

A Call to Surrender

That first sentence of mine is so familiar as, I am afraid, to have almost lost its meaning and its power. *Absolute surrender to Christ*: you have heard it over and over again. Great words have become divested of their meaning by constant use of them; and some of the great things of our speech have become discount and lack virtue.

What is absolute surrender to Christ? I am not talking to the man outside, who has never yet come into relationship to Christ, but to the man and the woman who share His life. What does absolute surrender to Christ mean? It is not admiration. You may admire the perfect beauty of the glorious Lord, and yet never become like Him. Not patronage. But can there be such a thing? I am afraid there can. I patronize Him when I speak of His glory in the pulpit unless I answer my speech in my life of obedience. There can be a great deal of patronage of the Lord Jesus Christ—sweet things said and sung about Him, great regard for His Name, following upon admiration for and testimony borne to intellectual convictions of His excellence—yet no approximation of life toward Him in likeness. That is not surrender.

I want to go one step further, and say that surrender to Christ does not mean imitation of Christ. It is the last desire in my heart to shock you; but that is another book I wish sometimes had never been written—the *Imitation of Christ*. If you have ever tried to imitate Him, you have found out how disastrous it was.

> How can I follow Him I serve?
> How can I copy Him I love?

I cannot copy Him; the surest way to discover it is to make the attempt. You may have tried honestly to imitate Him. You start in the morning, and you say, What would Jesus do? and you will fail before the day is out, if that is all. Surrender is not admiration; nor is it patronage; it is not even imitation.

What is it? Beloved, it is just *surrender*. That is what I mean by being hopeless in the presence of a great word. It is the absolute handing over of the life to the Christ. I will try to break it up a little. First, begin at the center of the life now—the will. Surrender to Christ means that I remit to His arbitration every choice that I make. It is not only the will, it is the intellect. Surrender to Christ means that I put into the fire of His pure love all my loves and my hates, that He may purify them; and that I have no hate save that which harmonizes with His hate, and no love save that which harmonizes with His love. These are hardly things for the platform and for the crowd, but for heart-searching. Here is what I am in the economy of God—a sharer of Christ's life, in preparation for ultimate vocation, taking an immediate responsibility. Massed against me are the hosts of wickedness; and they follow me everywhere; I can never escape them. How am I to fight so as to be equal to this?

The first thing is, I myself must be utterly at the disposal of the Christ who dwells within—the surrender of the life to the Indweller; and, in the particulars indicated, submitting to Him all my choices. Still I must choose, I must *elect* and *select*. I have to do it; it is part of my manhood, that for which God created me; but every choice must be remitted to Him. Is it so in my own life, in your life? As I often say, and today increasingly, I am not so much preaching to you as talking with you. Is it so with us? Do I ask to know His will before I go here or there? That is all; that is the first thing. And am I submitting to the mastery of Jesus Christ? I know that when a man says that, he is supposed to come into antagonism with what is called a great intellectual movement. I freely confess to you that Christ is such to me that I stand by what He says against all the scholars who have ever been born. I stand by His conceptions of God and of man, and of the Word of God, and of Himself in their relations to God and in their inter-relationships. And I feel that if we are to know this victory we must take that position—not merely submit to Him our will and ask His arbitration in our choices, but allow Him to be where He surely is: on the throne of our whole intellectual outlook.

In the third place, all the emotional nature must be submitted to the pure fire of His own love. You say, That means there will be no anger. It means nothing of the kind. If you are a Christian, you will be angry; but you will be angry in the right place, and with the right thing, and for the right reason. To my youngest friend I commend a simple Bible study—take the cases in the New Testament where it is said that Jesus was angry. I will tell you of one. He was angry when He said this: "Suffer the little children to come unto me, and forbid them not; for of such is the Kingdom of heaven." We recite that, and there is infinite winsomeness in our recitations; and accurately so, if we think of the children. But read it: do not take my word for it. "He was moved with indignation, and said unto them, Suffer the little children to come unto me." That is the reason for His indignation. You will find that to be the nature of His anger always; and all the anger in my life that is out of harmony with that anger is wrong, and sinful, and a hindrance. I must submit my emotional nature to Him, that He may come in and purify it.

A Call for Submission

Mark the next thing; and I speak of it with solemnity. I say that because so often we speak of it in terms of frivolity, I am afraid. *Your love must be submitted to Him.* Oh, the tragedies that lie all through the garden of God among His children because love—human love—has not been submitted to the test of His love. Oh, the men whose eyes flamed with missionary enthusiasm, whom you may discover money-grubbing in Babylon, because some girl crossed the path, and they did not submit their love to Christ. Oh, the daughters of the King, all beautiful within, who allowed their life to be blighted because they did not test love, when it came, in His presence. It is a sacred matter: do not refer to it idly or carelessly. I have seen such havoc wrought here.

Let me get back to the individual thing—surrender to Christ. All my choices submitted to Him, all my intellectual outlook under the mastery of His knowledge, and all my emotional nature for evermore resolutely brought to the test of His wonderful love, at the heart of which is the holiness of God—that, my brethren, in halting and imperfect description, is surrender to Christ. It is taking the whole of me, unlocking all the chambers, and saying, "O Christ, from now I will have no Lord but Thee, no Master but Thyself!" Surrender to Christ—and until that is so, there may be conflict and occasionally apparent victory; but the rule will be defeat and not victory. It is the wholly, the absolutely surrendered man, who knows what it is to say, "Having done all, to stand."

Patience under Discipline

For a moment, may I say that there must be not merely this surrender to Christ, but there must be now *patience under His discipline.* I want you to remember that, having surrendered, there is much to be done, "much land to be possessed"; and the indwelling Christ, in the moment when He has full right of way in all the life—volitional, intellectual, and emotional—leads and guides toward the correction of the center of the being.

Then there is the whole circumference to be brought under perfect control. It is possessed, but now has to be cultivated; and you and I have to be patient. There is to be the formation of the new habit. How is it so many imagine that in the Christian life habits come with a flash? They never do. In your old life, you formed habits of evil; a thing was done, and sometimes with difficulty, and then repeated until it became a habit, almost part of yourself. So in the new life, be patient. Be patient in the cultivation of fellowship and prayer, and power in prayer— all these things come at the beginning, in a certain sense; but there needs to be the patient and persistent cultivation of the habits of the new life, if there is to be victory in the presence of all the forces that are without.

The Spiritual Dimension

May I also say this in a sentence: *there must be cultivation of the neglected areas of your own life.* I am quite sure that all Christian workers have had this said to them in recent years. "Can you explain to me," I was asked by a Christian woman of culture and refinement, "how it is that my friends are excellent and beautiful people, without Christ?" I said, "Will you describe to me the excellence and the beauty?" "Yes," and she began to mention a great many things that are beautiful and excellent about refined people, and gentle people, and kind people. "Well," I said, "go on a little further. What is the difference between them and yourself?" Her answer was, "The difference is just this, that they never pray, never read the Bible, never worship."

"Now," I said, "the things you mention as lacking are the final things of beauty." When you have taken these people and have spoken of any refinement of beauty in them, you have spoken of the culture of that which is purely of the flesh. Mark well their attitude toward the lost, the suffering, and the sorrowing. You will discover that the final beauty of human life is the spiritual, which means first—and I dare to quote the words of Christ in this connection—love to God, and then love to your neighbor.

There is the peculiar and the final beauty of human life: right relationship to God—that which takes in eternity; recognizes Him; sees, far out beyond the horizon, the infinite distances, and turns back, with quick and ready sympathy, to touch the fallen and help bear their sorrows. This is utterly and absolutely missing in the case of all who do not know the Christ of God. We need to be patient in the cultivation of the neglected areas of our life. It is not easy to sit by the side of a lost woman, if you are a woman of refinement; but it may be made to present the chief delight of your life, repeating it as a habit to be performed. We need great patience with ourselves. I never say patience without thinking of another word at the heart of it—persistence. We need full surrender of the life to Christ, then patience and persistence in the cultivation of these things.

Fight as Well as Trust

And one other thing here. What is it? Definite, positive, actual *conflict*; and by that I mean resistance unto blood, striving against sin. How often the apostle would have that to say to us, would he not? Young people who profess to come into definite blessing here and elsewhere, presently come and say they have failed. Why? Was not the surrender genuine? Yes, it was sincere. Was there any lack of patience in attending to the details of Christ's training? Perhaps not. But over and over again, though the surrender has been sincere, and there has been patient endeavor, in some hour of crisis they have not fought; they have put up no fight.

A young fellow spoke to me yesterday and told of defeat after defeat. My dear boy, *you have to fight as well as trust.* A young man comes to my memory—suffer me to make the illustration—in whom I was profoundly and deeply interested some years ago; a man who was the slave of lust. He gave himself to Christ, as I verily believe, with all sincerity; and so far as he had light at the moment, he unlocked every chamber of his being, and Christ took possession. He set himself resolutely to patient endeavor under the discipline of the Lord. After about six months I missed him from his place, and went to seek him; and I shall never forget the almost rudeness with which he greeted me. "What do you want?" "I want you." "It's of no use coming to me." "Why not?" "Christ cannot save me." I looked at him; and beyond him I saw in his rooms, his "diggings" in London, certain pictures. I laid my hand on his shoulder, looked straight into his eyes, and said, "You are nothing short of a scamp." Sometimes you have to take men like that. "What do you mean?" "How dare you insult Christ that way? You tell me that Christ cannot save you. You have never given Him a chance. How long have those pictures been on your walls?" He hung his head, and said, "Oh, all the time." "And yet you tell me that Christ cannot save you! How have you been coming home from the city lately?" "Oh, well, with so-and-so." Exactly. No fight.

My brother, it is no use your coming to Keswick and submitting to Christ in some quiet hour here, unless you understand that now you have to stand and to withstand. There is to be the actual fight; and you begin that fight by burning every picture that hangs on your wall that ought not to be there; you begin that fight by going home five miles round, rather than go through the place of subtle and devilish temptation. It has to be an honest, manly fight. James gives the whole philosophy of the conflict: "Submit therefore to God, and resist the devil"—and if you submit and then never resist, the devil will win, just as surely as if you resist without submission the devil will win.

But listen: submit and resist, and having done all, you will stand. There is to be definite conflict against all the foes and forces that are without; and I warn you solemnly and of urgency against any conception of new blessing as that wherein you receive some mechanical power which will set you free from the necessity of definite conflict. Not so. But you can receive a power that will make you mighty to overcome against all the forces of hell if, surrendered, you submit to discipline and then enter into definite and positive conflict. The man who wrote this letter gave himself to Christ in a great abandonment on the Damascas road, when he said, "Lord, what wilt Thou have me to do?" That is submission. And then, with great patience and diligence through the years, he set himself to the discipline; he entered into definite conflict. And from beginning to end you catch the military tone whenever he speaks of his personal experiences in Christ Jesus.

Oh, brethren, do not forget the other—always the note of victory, the assurance of it. Blessed be God, mark this: when Paul came to the end of his career as a Christian apostle, a minister, and a missionary, he never sighs about failure in the ministry. "I have fought the good fight, I have kept the faith; henceforth there is laid up for me the crown of righteousness which the Lord, the righteous Judge, shall give me" (2 Tim. 4:8). And so that man who said, "Having done all, to stand," came to the end, and writing this letter in the first imprisonment of comparative ease, he wrote the last in the second imprisonment—the letter of Timothy—when everything seemed against him,

> With every note and every tone
> The note and tone of victory won—

but through conflict. Had he taken up the conflict in his own strength, he would have been defeated all the while; had he trusted only, with never a blow and never a conflict, he had been defeated.

"Having done all, to stand." Surrender, discipline, fight; and so the victory. I said at the commencement that theory and testimony are not a final demonstration to any soul. That I believe. Yet hear me now as I close: I have a theory, and I have a testimony. I will put my theory in these words: Christ cannot be defeated, and the man whom Christ has mastered is invincible. That is the theory. I have a testimony: and now hear it, and hear it carefully. What is my testimony? That my theory works. I know it. I make no apology for it; my boasting is in the Lord. I know that theory works. Then you mean to say, someone says, that you are claiming perfection? Do not misunderstand me. But I tell you what I have found out and do know: that whenever I am defeated, it is my own fault. It is a great thing to have found that out; it is a humbling thing, a searching thing. But thank God, I have found it out.

There was a day when I blamed my defeat on my environment. There sounded so much in that word; but I have given it up. God is the other environment. There was a day when I blamed my father for my failure. I have given it up. I hear Christian people quote the old adage, "The fathers have eaten sour grapes, and the children's teeth are set on edge." It is a lie. If your teeth are on edge, you have been at the sour grapes. But it is in the Bible! Oh, yes, a great many things are in the Bible. What for? To be contradicted, to be nailed down as false coin. Men, down by the waters of Babylon, were putting the blame on their fathers, and they said, "The fathers have eaten sour grapes, and the children's teeth are set on edge." And the answer was, "All souls are mine," says God. "Deal with me. Quit blaming your fathers; get into right relationship with me, and I will deliver."

And that is my message. I tell you, the theory works. And the proportion in which I have submitted, and do submit, to my Lord and Master, the proportion in which I am patient under His direction in learning the lines and the habits of the Christian life, the proportion in which I burn the bridges behind me and put up a fight—that is the proportion in which I win. Whenever I am defeated, it is either because I have locked some secret chamber against my Lord, or I have grown weary in the discipline, or else I have expected Him to fight while I watch. And along these lines defeat forever comes.

How to Find Victory

My last word is as my first. My testimony and my theory may serve—I pray God that they may, under the guidance of His Holy Spirit—as an inspiration; but they cannot demonstrate the truth to you. There you sit, still saying, "I wonder if it is true?" Exactly. That is the point. You say, "Here have I longed for this victory all along the way. Can it be?" That is it; you are asking the question. How shall you find out? Make the great adventure.

Forgive the crude way of putting it: I know no other at the moment—Give Christ His chance, by yielding yourself to Him. Supposing that no one has ever seen or known or lived the life—that is no argument against you making the adventure. You say, "If no man has lived the life, no man can live the life." If men on the lower level of life had acted upon such a theory as that, there would have been no discoveries made, no mountains climbed, no countries explored.

Young men, I call you to make the adventure. The ideal is a glorious one; the ideal of man with the light of eternity on his brow, with the Lord of eternity in his heart; the ideal of man walking through a world antagonistic to the things that are noble and pure, fighting against all the forces that oppose, and winning! It is a great ideal. I do not admit that no men have known the victory. The saints have known it in every age, in proportion as they were loyal to their Lord and Savior.

Where does it begin? I want to finish at the very center. Surrender to Christ. I am not talking to men and women who do not know Him. Trust Him. And now someone says, "Yes, yes; but that means—" I know. Do not tell anybody what you mean. You know; do not play the hypocrite. He never gives a man grace for two days ahead. "Lord, what wilt Thou have me to do?" said this man. "Go into Damascus, and it shall be told thee. . . ." That is the next thing. And you know the next—it is the friendship to be ended, the habit to be abandoned, that particular department of the business to be flung out. At one point He begins His administration; obey Him there, and He will move further in. But never forget this—I should not be true to the deepest conviction I have about life if I failed to say this—whenever He flings out, He never leaves a vacuum; He fills it. And the things He brings in as He clears others out, are the things of strength, and the things of beauty, and the things of joy. "Having done all, to stand."

God help us to make this great adventure, to give Him His opportunity by abandoning ourselves utterly and wholly to Him.

The Opposing Forces of the Religious Life—The Devil

George Campbell Morgan (1863-1945) was the son of a British Baptist preacher and preached his first sermon when he was 13 years old. He had no formal training for the ministry, but his tireless devotion to the study of the Bible helped him to become one of the leading Bible teachers of his day. Rejected by the Methodists, he was ordained into the Congregational ministry. He was associated with Dwight L. Moody in the Northfield Bible Conferences and as an itinerant Bible teacher. He is best known as the pastor of Westminster Chapel, London (1904-1917 and 1933-1945). During his second term there, he had Dr. D. Martyn Lloyd-Jones as his associate.

He published more than 60 books and booklets, and his sermons are found in *The Westminster Pulpit* (London, Pickering and Inglis). This sermon is from Volume 3.

George Campbell Morgan

6

THE OPPOSING FORCES OF THE RELIGIOUS LIFE—THE DEVIL

Submit yourselves therefore to God. Resist the devil, and he will flee from you   (James 4:7).

IN THIS STUDY, as in the previous ones, our appeal is made wholly to the Scriptures of truth. It is impossible to make such appeal and at the same time to deny the personality of Satan.

To deny the personality of Satan as revealed in the Scriptures is to have to believe that all the evil things with which we are familiar today, and all the dark and dastardly crimes of the centuries, have come out of human nature. This the Bible does not teach. There are two chapters at the commencement of the Bible and two at the end in which we have glimpses of this world unaffected by the devil. In the two first chapters he is not seen. In the last two chapters he is banished. Through the rest he is recognized and referred to as an actual personality of evil, and that to me is a most hopeful doctrine. If humanity is a part of God, then all murders and lies are part of the inactivity of God, and that is impossible of belief. I know it is not quite fashionable to talk about the devil today.

> Men don't believe in a devil now,
> As their fathers used to do;
> They reject one creed because it's old
> For another because it's new.
> There's not a print of his cloven foot,
> Nor a fiery dart from his bow,
> To be found in the earth or air today!
> At least—they declare it is so!
> But who is it mixes the fatal draught

That palsies heart and brain
And loads the bier of each passing year
With its hundred thousand slain?
But who blights the bloom of the land today
With the fiery breath of hell?
If it isn't the devil that does the work,
Who does? Won't somebody tell?
Who dogs the step of the toiling saint?
Who spreads the net for his feet?
Who sows the tares in the world's broad field
Where the Savior sows His wheat?
If the devil is voted not to be,
Is the verdict therefore true?
Someone is surely doing the work
The devil was thought to do.
They may say the devil has never lived,
They may say the devil is gone;
But simple people would like to know
Who carries the business on.

The Devil Revealed in Scripture

The personality of Satan is revealed as distinctly in the New Testament as is the personality of Jesus Christ. To deny the one is to deny the other. In casting out demons Christ perpetually addressed Himself to them as to definite personalities, possessing men, and all through that New Testament story it is quite evident that the personality of the devil was believed in.

But now what does the Bible teach concerning this personality? First of all, the Bible never suggests that Satan is self-existent; and if not self-existent, therefore created; and if created, created by God. God creates everything good, and nothing evil. "Do not I, the Lord, create evil?" is a distinct declaration of Scripture, but read the context, and it is at once seen that the word "evil" there means calamity, judgment on a guilty city. Therefore it is perfectly evident that, according to Bible teaching, Satan being not self-existent, but created, and that by God, was therefore created good. And if today he is evil, he has fallen from his original estate.

There was a time when the disciples came back to Jesus, and said, "Even the devils are subject to us." and there fell from the lips of the Master these very remarkable words, "I beheld Satan as lightning fall from heaven" (Luke 10:18). There a whole history is condensed into a flash; and a great unveiling of truth comes almost with a blinding glare. The disciples said, Even the demons are subject to us, and Christ's answer in effect was this, You need not be surprised that demons are subject unto you in My name. Satan, himself, the prince of the hosts of wickedness, the lord of the whole empire of sin, is not enthroned, he is fallen from heaven. It is testimony borne by the lips of Christ to a primal fall; to the fact that Satan is one of the principalities, one of the powers, an angel, but an angel fallen as lightning from heaven.

There is very little doubt that Peter heard that word of Jesus, and when I turn to his epistles I find in the course of an argument he declared, "For if God spared not angels that sinned, but cast them down to hell, and delivered them into chains of darkness, to be reserved unto judgment" (2 Peter 2:4). That is an inspired declaration of the fact that God spared not angels when they sinned, but cast them down, committed them to pits of darkness.

Jude, in his brief epistle, gives us a still more detailed and remarkable account of the primal fall of angels. Hear these words, "Angels which kept not their own principality, but left their proper habitation" (v. 6). The Authorized Version reads, "their first estate." Which is the better translation I cannot tell. I should be inclined to change them both and read, "Angels which kept not true to first principles, left their proper habitation or residence, or sphere, or orbit, He hath kept in everlasting bonds under darkness unto the judgment of the great day." There is nothing detailed in all this, but there is quite sufficient to reveal all that it is necessary for us to know. It is the story of a fall of angels led by one. Jesus named the one in the forefront, the leader, "I beheld *Satan* as lightning fall from heaven." Peter writes in the plural, "God spared not the angels that sinned, but cast them down to hell, and (committed them) to chains of darkness." Jude went a little more carefully into the matter and declared that they "kept not their own principality." They were not true to the principle of their own life, they left their proper orbit, habitation, residence, sphere, but they did not escape from Divine government when they so fell. He kept them "in everlasting bonds under darkness unto the judgment of the great day."

What was the sin? Who shall dare to say? In Milton's "Paradise Lost" we have splendid speculation as to what the sin was; and in all probability more than speculation.

Satan is never spoken of as having any independent existence. He is never spoken of as having sovereign dominion. The Bible never suggests that he has successfully cast off the government of God: He is in rebellion against it, but still held by it. That is the meaning of the petition in the Lord's prayer, "Bring us not into temptation, but deliver us from evil." It is a recognition of the fact that the very forces of evil in the spiritual realm are still under the government of God. To imagine that the Bible teaches against God successfully, is to contradict entirely what the Bible perpetually teaches.

Now notice what this means. The devil is not omnipotent. The devil is not omniscient. The devil is not omnipresent. Let me begin with the last first. The Bible never suggests the omnipresence of the devil. Someone says, The devil is here. How do you know? You have no proof of it. It is impossible for the devil to be in London and in New York at the same moment. To admit the creation of angels is to admit limitation and location. Whether you think of angels fallen or unfallen, I pray you remember none of them is omnipresent. They come, they go. They guard and watch the saints, for "Are they not all ministering spirits, sent forth to minister for them who shall be heirs of salvation?" (Heb. 1:11). So also with Satan and all the fallen angels, none of them are omnipresent. The number of them is so great that in every assembly, and over every man, some of them watch in order to destroy. But Satan himself, marshaling, guiding, commanding the hosts of spiritual wickedness, can never be in two places at once. Swifter than the lightning's flash, quicker than the thought of man can travel, he may encircle the globe, but he is not omnipresent. He is personal only in the measure in which any angel is personal. He is personal only in the measure in which man is personal.

Neither is he omniscient, knowing everything, seeing the end from the beginning, as God is able to do. Far more subtle in his wisdom, far more keen in his intuitions, far cleverer than man has ever been, but certainly not seeing all the ultimate issue from the commencement. And assuredly he is not omnipotent, not having all power. Go to the Book of Job, and put all that wonderful story into brief words in this respect. The devil, full of subtlety, and malice, and determination to spoil the work of God in the human soul, could nevertheless not touch a single hair upon the back of a single camel belonging to Job until he had asked God's leave.

The protest against dualism is out of place when you are thinking of the devil, according to Scripture teaching. The protest may be a very excellent one according to much misinterpretation of Scripture teaching which has possessed or obsessed the minds of men. If you once deny the existence of the devil in the universe because God is all and in all, that is to postulate a doctrine of the universe which is unscriptural. That doctrine must equally deny the existence of man. Is man a personality? If you admit that he is, then you may also admit the possibility of a personality in the universe other than God, created by God, who in some way is out of harmony with God, is indeed in antagonism against God, and yet who is not coequal with God in power, or in knowledge, or in presence.

Now, for a moment take the other side of this matter, and think of his power as revealed in the Scriptures of truth. Do not forget that he is spiritual in essence. All the angels are spirits, flames of fire, and Satan, one of the hierarchy of heaven, fallen, is a spirit. If it be true, as Tennyson says, that "Spirit with spirit can meet," referring to man's possibility of approaching God, it is equally true that the devil as spirit and man as spirit can meet, and in that fact lies the tremendous power of Satan, and of all those hosts that he commands, the army of fallen angels that are spiritual in essence.

Then also he is subtle in method. "Subtle" seems a weak word to use in connection with the devil. Paul describes the devil as an "angel of light." Peter describes the devil as a "roaring lion." Jesus refers to him as "the prince of this world." Each description suggests a different method, adopted according to the occasion, and according to the purpose—transforming himself into an angel of light to deceive if it be possible the very elect, appearing in awful ferocity and fierceness as a roaring lion to overwhelm the timid and afraid; the prince of the world offering to man all the kingdoms for a moment's homage, coming to men according to the method necessary to entrap them and spoil them, and harm them. This is awful sublety.

Then, again, he is revealed in Scripture as being strenuous in enterprise and stupendous in execution. He is the leader of vast hosts. Paul says, "We wrestle not against flesh and blood, but against principalities, against powers, against the rulers of the darkness, against spiritual wickedness in high places" (Eph. 6:12). That is a graphic description of this army of spiritual forces fighting against everything that is in harmony with the will of God. Those of us who accept the teaching of Scripture as final, recognize the place of angels fallen and unfallen. At the head of fallen angels, marshaling all, is the great head and center, the mightiest of them, the wisest of them, the most wonderful of them, his might, his wisdom, and his wonder prostituted in the universe of God to the purpose of fighting against God and yet forevermore held in check and never allowed to pass the limit of the government of God.

The Devil as Opposed to Religion

Now consider what is taught in Scripture concerning the devil as opposed to religion. All I have attempted to say concerning him as revealed in Scripture makes it patent that he must be and is the enemy of religion. Let us again appeal to Scripture for his character in relation to man. Jesus said concerning him, "He was a murderer from the beginning, and abode not in the truth, because there is no truth in him. When he speaketh a lie, he speaketh of his own: for he is a liar, and the father of it" (John 8:44).

A lie is essential evil. Jesus said, "I am the Truth," that is, essential good. A lie is the direct opposite. The original lie in human history was a denial of the creature's relation to God, and a suggestion in the heart of man that God was hard, unkind, capricious, prompting man to rebellion against Him.

If I come to the writings of the Apostle John, I read that he thus describes Satan, "The evil one." That is a term that describes him absolutely. He is the very embodiment of sin. Let me take you to three other descriptive words in order that we may see how he is opposed to religion. He is described as "the god of this world," as "the prince of the world," as "the prince of the power of the air, the spirit that now worketh in the children of disobedience" (Eph. 2:2). Put these three descriptions together and you will see that in this wonderful personality of evil, mastering the hosts of evil, there is the exact antithesis of all we know of God—One, "God and Father"; the other, "the god of this world"; one, "God the Son"; the other, "the prince of the world"; one, "God the Holy Spirit"; the other, "the prince of the power of the air, of the spirit that now worketh in the children of disobedience."

Thus in this personality there reside all the things that are opposed to the things in God. In God the Father there is essential government, in "the god of this world" there is disorder, evil. In God the Son there is grace, and in the devil there is essential disorder, evil. In God the Son there is grace, and in the devil there is everything opposed to grace. In God the Holy Spirit there is guidance for the sons of men and for the world: the devil is forevermore leading men away from the true path out into the desert and out into darkness. He is not coequal with God, but in the measure of his personality he is antagonistic to God, to His government, to His grace, to His guidance, forevermore trying to lead men astray.

"The god of this world." The world is devil-governed until this hour. Go to the homes of darkness in the far distant places of the world, and you will see that the fact is awfully patent. Are our big cities governed by our God? Is love the master principle of human life? If not, then what? This. It is each for himself, and the devil take the hindmost. Men are under the government of Satan. Through all that great and remarkable antithesis the devil is seen, not coequal with God, not omnipotent, omniscient, or omnipresent, but a fallen seraph, far more wondrous in wisdom than any son of man, with more subtle and marvelous power than man has ever yet possessed, marshaling the great hosts of fallen angels, and fighting against all the things that are in the will of God.

It becomes evident that he is the active and awful enemy of any man who begins to live the religious life in the true sense of the word. God loves man, and therefore the devil hates man because the devil is against God. God loves Christ in man, and therefore the devil hates Christ in man, and will prevent, if he can, the outworking of the Christ life in human character. Christ's mission was "to destroy the works of the devil." The devil's mission was to prevent that, and to destroy the works of Christ.

If I am beginning to live the life that is obedient to God's rule, the life of loyalty to Christ, the life in which the purposes of Christ and the plans of Christ and the power of Christ are present, then immediately I become one against whom the devil, either in actual person or through those who serve under him, is at war. The young Christian asks, How is it I am being tempted as I was never tempted before? There is the answer. Because the moment in which you turned your life back again toward God you became one against whom the devil is at war.

That is the declared fact in the passage to which I have made so many references, "We wrestle not against flesh and blood, but against principalities, against powers . . ." (Eph. 6:12). This is the terrible fact, and the man who does not face the fact is a fool. Our enemy patiently waits for the moment of weakness and is utterly merciless. It was a terrific word written in the book of Job, "Hast thou considered My servant Job?" There is a whole revelation of the devil's method in that word "*considered*"—watching for the opportunity of weakness and the place where to break in. The chain is only as strong as its weakest link, and the castle is only as strong as its least guarded door, and the devil is watching for the weak link, and for the least guarded door. There are men he will never tempt with a glass of wine, because a glass of wine is no temptation to them. Your least guarded door, your weakest link, pride, or passion, or lust, the intellectual, the emotional, the volitional, he is watching. Mark the awfulness of the figure, w*atching*. "Hast thou *considered* My servant Job?"

The Word, the Flesh and the Devil

It is against this enemy that we have to fight. That leads me to a brief word on the devil in relation to the world and the flesh. These are the media through which he acts, and in which he hides. You can find only one great occasion in all human history when the devil came out into the open. That was when in the wilderness he met Jesus Christ. He was not in the open in the Garden of Eden. He did not for a moment suggest that man should fall down and worship him there. What he said was, Please yourself! He suggested that man should leave the first principles of his life as the devil had left his, and depart from his proper habitation as the devil had departed from his. Is not that the primal sin? Is not that the sin of Lucifer, the son of the morning? Is not that the heart and center of all evil, self-pleasing?

The devil hid himself. So he does today. In the middle ages the devil was portrayed by artists as with horns and hoofs. If you paint him so today no one will know him. Marie Corelli, in her *Sorrows of Satan*, gives her last picture of the devil going into the House of Commons. If he ever makes any appearance in London, that is far nearer the truth than the horns and hoofs. That is part of his strategy, part of his subtlety. He is hiding today in half our theology and in half our new-fangled philosophies.

We are told today that man has to fight against the beast in him, that there are angel and beast in him, and that if the angel in him will fight hard enough he will trample the beast under his feet. There is an element of truth in all that. But what has turned man into a beast? Lurking behind the flesh, making it the medium of his suggestion, is the devil. Once I say he was dragged into the open, and advisedly I say *dragged*. If the devil could have escaped that ordeal he would have.

Jesus was driven of the Spirit into the wilderness to be tempted of the devil, led of the Spirit in the wilderness while being tempted of the devil. God dragged the devil out into the open. It is an appalling picture of the subtlety and power of the devil, but it also reveals the fact that all the artifice and subtlety of the devil is helpless when a man stands squarely on the will of God, and makes it the master passion of his life.

Take the story of the temptation and consider it carefully, and you will see the limitation of the devil. He has only three avenues along which he can ever approach the citadel of man's soul, and they are all revealed there. The real enemy that we have to fight is not the beast in us, but the devil behind the beast. It is not the flesh and the world but the devil's misrepresentation of the world: "The god of this world hath blinded their eyes." The archenemy, the master enemy, the one real foe of their religious life, is the devil and all the hosts that he commands.

The Way of Victory

Are we to be defeated by this foe? The apostle in the passage I read to you recognizes the conflict, *"we wrestle."* It is very definite conflict. We are to put on the whole panoply of God, we are to stand, to withstand, and having done all to stand. So the victory is possible according to the apostle's outlook. If you ask me the way of victory, I take you back again to a passage which puts the whole truth into simplest form. James said, "Submit . . . to God. Resist the devil, and he will flee from you" (James 4:7). Submit! There is deep reason for this. It gets down to the root of the whole matter. The devil's sin was rebellion, and his method with man is to propose rebellion, and the moment a man submits to God he crosses the devil's plan and purpose. The idea is that of a soldier. Submission is the first law of success in warfare. There can be no ultimate victory save under discipline and submission.

What next? "Resist." After you have submitted to God there will be conflict, but the conflict will be under orders, under the command of One Who knows every method of the enemy, Who holds in His own hand the reins of ultimate government. So that the conflict will no longer be in unexpected places. We sing about the devil being ambushed, but God knows where he is ambushed. The man who is really submitted to God starts out to real difficult conflict, strenuous fight, but he is under the command of One Who is never caught unawares, Who knows the whole field, the whole plan of the foe, Who never lost a battle, and Who never will, Whose soldier never will, so long as he obeys, and so long as he follows.

Note James' confident assertion, "Submit . . . to God; resist the devil, and he will flee from you." That is the way of victory. I cannot add anything to it. Indeed, I am inclined to think that in any attempt to add I am in great danger of subtracting from the force and power of the simple statement. Submit and resist.

Someone says, but I fail and fall. I hear the voice and I yield, I sin; why do I sin? Because you have not obeyed this method, Submit, and resist. I have known men who have submitted seriously, earnestly, sincerely, but they have fallen. Why? *They did not add to submission resistance.* I have known other men who have resisted, who are resisting, and they say, How is it I am beaten? I have put up this fight against the devil, and I am down again. You did not begin your resistance by *submitting.* If a man submits and never fights, God will not, cannot, lead him to victory. If a man fights without having submitted, he has not put himself under discipline, under orders, and he will be beaten.

Or you submitted but never fought. The word of the writer of the letter to the Hebrews is very striking, "You have not yet resisted unto blood, striving against sin" (12:4). You submitted but there was no resistance, you did not burn your bridges behind you. You locked the whiskey up in a cupboard in case you should need it some day, and you were drunk in a month. There was no fight. You kept the impure picture in your own private cupboard and you were back in your devilish licentiousness within a week. You have to put up a fight. Put yourself under control, act under the Captain's orders. Submit now, and resist the moment the devil meets you. That way lies victory. The quaint old hymn which we never sing now is nevertheless true if it be rightly interpreted:

> Satan trembles when he sees
> The weakest saint upon his knees.

I said, when it is rightly interpreted. If you get on your knees and do not fight, Satan is not at all afraid of you. If you know what it is to get to your knees and gather strength, and then fight, all the forces of the fallen intelligences are not wise enough, and all their might is not strong enough, to overcome you. *Submit, resist.* Let the two words abide with us as we part.

NOTES

The Sword of the Spirit

Charles Haddon Spurgeon (1834-1892) is undoubtedly the most famous minister of modern times. Converted in 1850, he united with the Baptists and soon began to preach in various places. He became pastor of the Baptist church in Waterbeach in 1851, and three years later he was called to the decaying Park Street Church, London. Within a short time, the work began to prosper, a new church was built and dedicated in 1861, and Spurgeon became London's most popular preacher. In 1855, he began to publish his sermons weekly; and today they make up the fifty-seven volumes of *The Metropolitan Pulpit*. He founded a pastor's college and several orphanages.

This sermon is taken from *The Metropolitan Tabernacle Pulpit*, volume 37, and was preached on Sunday morning, April 19, 1891.

Charles Haddon Spurgeon

7

THE SWORD OF THE SPIRIT

Take the sword of the Spirit, which is the word of
God (Ephesians 6:17).

TO BE A CHRISTIAN is to be warrior. The good soldier of
Jesus Christ must not expect to find ease in this world: it
is a battlefield. Neither must he reckon upon the friendship
of the world for that would be enmity against God. His
occupation is war. As he puts on piece by piece of the
panoply provided for him, he may wisely say to himself,
"This warns me of danger; this prepares me for warfare;
this prophesies opposition."

Difficulties meet us even in standing our ground for the
apostle, two or three times, bids us—"Stand." In the rush
of the fight, men are apt to be carried off their legs. If they
can keep their footing, they will be victorious; but if they
are borne down by the rush of their adversaries, everything is lost. You are to put on the heavenly armor in
order that you may stand; and you will need it to maintain the position in which your Captain has placed you. If
even to stand requires all this care, judge ye what the
warfare must be! The apostle also speaks of *withstanding*
as well as standing. We are not merely to defend, but also
to assail. It is not enough that you are not conquered, you
have to conquer. Hence we find that we are to take not
only a helmet to protect the head, but also a sword with
which to annoy the foe. Ours, therefore, is a stern conflict,
standing and withstanding; and we shall want all the
armor from the divine magazine, all the strength from
the mighty God of Jacob.

It is clear from our text that our defense and our
conquest must be obtained by sheer fighting. Many try
compromise; but if you are a true Christian, you can
never do this business well. The language of deceit fits

not a holy tongue. The adversary is the father of lies, and those who are with him understand the art of equivocation; but saints abhor it. If we discuss terms of peace, and attempt to gain something by policy, we have entered upon a course from which we shall return in disgrace. We have no order from our Captain to patch up a truce and get as good terms as we can. We are not sent out to offer concessions. It is said that if we yield a little, perhaps the world will yield a little also, and good may come of it. If we are not too strict and narrow, perhaps sin will kindly consent to be more decent. Our association with it will prevent its being so barefaced and atrocious. If we are not narrow-minded, our broad doctrine will go down with the world, and those on the other side will not be so greedy of error as they now are. No such thing. Assuredly this is not the order which our Captain has issued. When peace is to be made, He will make it Himself, or He will tell us how to behave to that end; but at present our orders are very different.

Neither may we hope to gain by being neutral or granting an occasional truce. We are not to cease from conflict and try to be as agreeable as we can with our Lord's foes, frequenting their assemblies and tasting their dainties. No such orders are written here. You are to grasp your weapon and go forth to fight.

Neither may you so much as dream of winning the battle by accident. No man was ever holy by a happy chance. Infinite damage may be done by carelessness; but no man ever won life's battle by it. To let things go on as they please is to let them bear us down to hell. We have no orders to be quiet and take matters easily. No; we are to pray always and watch constantly. The one note that rings out from the text is this—*Take the sword! Take the sword!* No longer is it talk and debate! No longer is it parley and compromise! The word of thunder is—*Take the sword!* The Captain's voice is clear as a trumpet— *Take the sword!* No Christian man here will have been obedient to our text unless with clear, sharp, and decisive firmness, courage, and resolve, he takes the sword. We must go to heaven sword in hand, all the way. *"Take the sword.*" On this command I would enlarge. May the Holy Spirit help me!

It is noteworthy that there is only one weapon of offense provided, although there are several pieces of armor. The Roman soldier usually carried a spear as well as a sword. We have seen frequent representations of the legionary standing upon guard as sentry, and he almost always stands with a spear in his right hand while his sword hangs at his side. But Paul, for excellent reasons, concentrates our offensive weapon in one because it answers for all. We are to use *the sword*, and that only. Therefore, if you are going to this fight, see well to your only weapon. If you are to have no other, take care that you have this always in your hand. Let the Captain's voice ring in your ear, *"Take the sword! Take the sword!"*, and so go forth to the field.

The Sword Is the Word

Notice, first, *the sword you are to take is the sword of the Spirit, which is the Word of God.* That is our first head; and the second is equally upon the surface of the text: *This sword is to be ours.* We are ordered to take the sword of the Spirit, and so make it our own sword.

First, the Word of God which is to be our one weapon is of noble origin, for it is "the sword of the Spirit." It has the properties of a sword, and those were given it by the Spirit of God.

Here we note that *the Holy Spirit has a sword.* He is quiet as the dew, tender as the anointing oil, soft as the zephyr of eventide, and peaceful as a dove; and yet, under another aspect, He wields a deadly weapon. He is the Spirit of judgment and the Spirit of burning, and He beareth not the sword in vain. Of Him it may be said, "The Lord is a man of war: Jehovah is his name."

The Word of God in the hand of the Spirit wounds very terribly, and makes the heart of man to bleed. Do you not remember, some of you, when you used to be gashed with this sword Sunday after Sunday? Were you not cut to the heart of it so as to be angry with it? You almost made up your mind to turn away from hearing the gospel again. That sword pursued you, and pierced you in the secrets of your soul, and made you bleed in a thousand places. At last you were "pricked in the heart," which is a far better thing than being "cut to the heart"; and then execution was done, indeed. That wound was deadly, and none but He that killed could make you alive. Do you recollect how, after this, your sins were slain one after another? Their necks were laid on the block, and the Spirit acted as an executioner with His sword. The Word gave you life; but it was at the first a great killer. Your soul was like a battlefield after a great fight, under the first operations of the divine Spirit, whose sword returns not empty from the conflict.

Beloved, the Spirit of God has war with the Amalek of evil and error from generation to generation. He will spare none of the evils which now pollute the nations; His sword will never be quiet till all these Canaanites are destroyed. The Holy Spirit glorifies Christ not only by what He reveals, but also by what He overturns. The strife may be weary, but it will be carried on from age to age, till the Lord Jesus shall appear; forever shall the Spirit of God espouse the cause of love against hate, of truth against error, of holiness against sin, of Christ against Satan. He will win the day, and those who are with Him shall in His might be more than conquerors. The Holy Spirit has proclaimed war and wields a two-edged sword.

The Holy Spirit wields no sword but the Word of God. This wonderful Book, which contains the utterances of God's mouth, is the one weapon which the Holy Spirit elects to use for His warlike purposes. It is a spiritual weapon and so is suitable to the Holy Spirit. The weapons of His warfare are not carnal. He never uses either persecution or patronage, force or bribery, glitter of grandeur, or terror of power. He works upon men by the Word, which is suitable to His own spiritual nature, and to the spiritual work which is to be accomplished. While it is spiritual, this weapon is "mighty through God." A cut from the Word of God will cleave a man's spirit from head to foot; so sharp is this sword. Though by long practice in sin a man may have coated himself as with mail impenetrable, yet the Word of the Lord will divide the northern iron and the steel.

The Holy Spirit can make a man feel the divine power of the sacred Word in the very center of His being. For battling with the spirits of man, or with spirits of an infernal kind, there is no weapon so keen, so piercing, so able to divide between the joints and marrow, so penetrating as to the thoughts and intents of the heart. In the Spirit's hand, the Word gives no flesh-wound, but cuts into the man's heart, and so wounds him that there is no healing save by supernatural power. The wounded conscience will bleed; its pains will be upon it day and night; and though it seek out a thousand medicines, no salve but one can cure a gash which this terrible sword has made. This weapon is two-edged; indeed, it is all edge; and whichever way it strikes, it wounds and kills. There is no such thing as the flat of the sword of the Spirit—it has a razor edge every way. Beware how you handle it, you critics; it may wound even you: it will cut you to your destruction, one of these days, except you be converted. He that uses the Word in the Lord's battles may use it upon carnal hopes and then strike back upon unbelieving fears; he may smite with one edge the love of sin, and then with the other the pride of self-righteousness. It is a conquering weapon in all ways, this wondrous sword of the Spirit of God.

The Word, we say, is the only sword which the Spirit uses. I know the Holy Spirit uses gracious sermons; but it is only in proportion as they have the Word of God in them. I know the Holy Spirit uses religious books; but only so far as they are the Word of God told out in other language. Conviction, conversion, and consolation still are wrought, but only by the Word of God. Learn, then, the wisdom of using the Word of God for holy purposes. The Spirit has abundant ability to speak of His own self, apart from the Written Word. The Holy Spirit is God, and therefore He is the greatest spirit in the universe. All wisdom dwells in Him. He thought out the laws which govern nature and direct providence. The Holy Spirit is the great teacher of human spirits. He taught Bezaleel and the artificers in the wilderness how to make the fine linen, and the gold and carved work for the tabernacle. All arts and sciences are perfectly known to Him, and infinitely more than men can ever discover. Yet He will not use those things in this holy controversy. In the quarrel of His covenant He neither uses philosophy, nor science, nor rhetoric. In contending against the powers of darkness, "The sword of the Spirit is the Word of God." "It is written" is His master-stroke. Words which God has spoken by holy men of old, and has caused to be recorded on the sacred page—these are the battle-ax and weapons of war of His Spirit. This Book contains the Word of God, and is the Word of God; and this it is which the Holy Spirit judges to be so effectual a weapon against evil that He uses this, and this only, as His sword in the great conflict with the powers of darkness.

The Word is the sword of the Spirit because it is of His own making. He will not use a weapon of human workmanship, lest the sword boast itself against the hand that wields it. The Holy Spirit revealed the mind of God to the minds of holy men; He spoke the word into their hearts, and thus He made them think as He would have them think, and to write what He willed them to write so that what they spoke and wrote was spoken and written as they were moved by the Holy Spirit. Blessed be the Holy Spirit for deigning to use so many writers, and yet Himself to remain the veritable Author of this collection of holy books. We are grateful for Moses, for David, for Isaiah, for Paul, for Peter, for John, but most of all for that superintending Editor, that innermost Author of the whole sacred volume—even the Holy Spirit.

A warrior may well be careful as to the make of his sword. If a man had made his own sword, had tempered the metal, had himself passed the blade through many fires, and wrought it to perfection, then, if he were a skillful workman, he would feel confidence in his sword. When work is done nowadays, it is, as a rule, badly done. Work done by contract is usually scamped in some part or another; but when a man does a work for himself he is likely to do it thoroughly, and produce an article which he can depend upon. The Holy Spirit has made this Book Himself; every portion of it bears His initial and impress; and thus He has a sword worthy of His own hand, a true Jerusalem blade of heavenly fabric. He delights to use a weapon so divinely made, and He does use it right gloriously.

The Word of God is also the sword of the Spirit because He puts the edge upon it. It is because He is in it that it is so keen and cutting. I believe in the inspiration of Holy Scripture, not only in the day when it was written, but onward, and even to this day. It is still inspired; the Holy Spirit still breathes through the chosen words. I told you the sword was all edge; but I would add that the Holy Spirit makes it so. It would have no edge at all if it were not for His presence within it, and His perpetual working by it.

How many people read their Bibles, and yet derive no more benefit therefrom than if they had read an old almanac! In fact, they would more easily keep awake over an ancient old book than over a chapter of Scripture. The ministers of the gospel may preach God's Word in all sincerity and purity, and yet, if the Spirit of God be not present, we might as well have preached mere moral essays, for no good can come of our testimony.

The Holy Spirit rides in the chariot of Scripture and not in the wagon of modern thought. Scripture is that ark of the covenant which contains the golden pot of manna, and also bears above it the divine light of God's shining. The Spirit of God works in, by, and through, and with the Word; and if we keep to that Word, we may rest assured that the Holy Spirit will keep with us, and make our testimony to be a thing of power. Let us pray the blessed Spirit to put an edge on our preaching, lest we say much and accomplish little. Hear us in this thing, O blessed One!

It is "the sword of the Spirit" because *He alone can instruct us in the use of it.* You think, young man, that you can pick up your Bible, and go and preach from it at once, properly and successfully. You have made a presumptuous mistake. A sword is a weapon which may do hurt to the man who flourishes with it in mere wanton pride. No one can handle the sword of the Spirit aright save the chosen man whom God has ordained from before the foundation of the world and trained in feats of arms. By this the elect of God are known—that they love the

Word of God, and they have a reverence for it and discern between it and the words of man.

Notice the lambs in the field, just now; and there may be a thousand ewes and lambs; but every lamb finds out its own mother. So does a true-born child of God know where to go for the milk which is to nourish his soul. The sheep of Christ know the Shepherd's voice in the Word, and a stranger will they not follow, for they know the voice of strangers. God's own people have discernment to discover and relish God's own Word. They will not be misled by the cunning craftiness of human devices. Saints know the Scriptures by inward instinct.

The holy life, which God has infused into believers by His Spirit, loves the Scriptures, and learns how to use them for holy purposes. Young soldier, you must go to the training-ground of the Holy Spirit to be made a proficient swordsman. You will go in vain to the metaphysician or to the logician, for neither of these knows how to handle a spiritual weapon. In other arts they may be masters; but in the sacred use of divine theology they are mere fools. In the things of the Word we are dunces till we enter the school of the Holy Spirit. He must take of the things of Christ and show them unto us. He must teach us how to grip this sword by faith, and how to hold it by watchfulness, so as to parry the adversary's thrust, and carry the war into the foeman's territory.

He is well taught who can swing this great two-handed sword to and fro, and mow a lane through the midst of his opponents, and come out a conqueror at the end. It may take a long time to learn this art; but we have a right skillful Teacher. Those of us who have been in this warfare thirty or forty years feel that we have not yet reached the full use of this sword; nay, I know for one, that I need daily to be taught how to use this mysterious weapon which is capable of so much more than I have yet supposed. It is the sword of the Spirit, adapted for the use of an Almighty arm, and therefore equal to the doing of far more than we think. Holy Spirit, teach us new feats of arms by this thy sword!

But, chiefly, it is the sword of the Spirit, because *He is the great Master in the use of it.* Oh, that He would come and show us how He can thrust and cleave with it! In this house of prayer we have often seen Him at His work. Here the slain of the Lord have been many. We have seen this sword take off the head of many a Goliath doubt, and slay a horde of cares and unbeliefs. We have seen the Spirit pile up heaps on heaps of the slain when the Word of conviction has gone forth, and men have seen sin to be sin, and fallen down as dead before the Lord and His law. We also know what the use of the sword by the Spirit of God means, for within our own being He has left marks of His prowess. He has killed our doubts and fears and left no more mistrusts to worry us.

There was a man of God who was frequently subject to doubts, even doubts upon the fundamentals of religion. He hated this state of mind; but still he could not get rid of the habit of evil questioning. In answer to prayer, the Spirit came, and convinced him of the pride of his intellect, and of the wickedness of setting up his judgment against the Word of the Lord; and from that day forward he was never the subject of another fit of unbelief. He saw things clearly in the light of the Holy Spirit; and that is to see them indeed. The great giant of doubt is sorely wounded by the sword of the Spirit—yea, he is slain outright; for the Spirit works in the believer such a conviction of the truth that assurance banishes suspicion.

When the Holy Spirit deals with the lusts of the flesh, and the lusts of the eye and the pride of life, these also lie at His feet, trophies to the power of His mighty weapon, even the Word of God! The Holy Spirit is glorious in the use of this sword. He finds that this weapon suits His hand, and He seeks no other. Let us use it also, and be glad to do so. Though it is the sword of the Spirit, yet our feebler hand may grasp it; yea, and find in the grasping that somewhat of the divine power comes unto our arm.

Fellow believers, is it not a very high honor put upon you, as soldiers of the cross, that you should be allowed, even commanded to take the sword of the Spirit? The raw recruit is not trusted with the general's sword; but here are you armed with the weapon of God the Holy

Spirit, and called upon to bear that sacred sword which is so gloriously wielded by the Lord God Himself. This we are to bear, and no other. Does the timid heart inquire, "Wherewithal, my Master, shall I meet my adversaries"? "Here," says the Holy Spirit, "take this!" This is my own sword; I have done great with it; take it, and nothing shall stand against you." When you remember the potency of this sword, when the Spirit tests it upon yourself, you may take it with confidence, and use it in your holy war with full assurance. That Word of God which could convert *you*, can convert anybody; if it could kill your despair, it can remove another man's despondency; if it has conquered your pride and self-will, it can subdue the like in your children and your neighbors. Having done what it has certainly done for you, you may have a full persuasion that, before its power, no case is hopeless. Wherefore, see to it, that you use from this day forth no other weapon than the sword of the Spirit, which is the Word of God.

The Sword Is Ours

This fairly lands me in the second portion of my discourse. The Word of God is the sword of the Spirit; but *it is also to be our sword.*

Here I must begin again, and go over much the same ground. *We shall need a sword.* Our warfare is not child's play: we mean business. We have to deal with fierce foes who are only to be met with keen weapons. Buffets will not suffice in this contest; we must come to sword-cuts. You may be of a very quiet spirit, but your adversaries are not so. If you attempt to play at Christian warfare, they will not. To meet the powers of darkness is no sham battle. They mean mischief. Nothing but your eternal damnation will satisfy the fiendish hearts of Satan and his crew. You must take not so much a flag to unfurl, or a drum to beat, as a sword to use, and a specially sharp sword too. In this combat you will have to use a sword such as even evil spirits can feel, capable of dividing asunder of soul and spirit, and of the joints and marrow. If you are to live through this fight, and come off victorious, no form of conflict will suffice less sharp and cutting than sword-work.

Depend upon it that in this struggle you will be forced to come to close quarters. The foe aims at your heart and pushes home. A spear will not suffice, nor bow and arrow; the enemy is too near for anything but hand-to-hand fighting. Our foes are not only of our house, but of our heart. I find an enemy within which is always near, and I cannot get away from him. I find that my antagonist will get his hand on my throat if he can. If our foes were far away, and we could play upon them with artillery which would kill at six or seven miles' distance, we might lead a pretty easy life. But no; they are *here!* At our doors! Yea, within us; nearer than hands and feet.

Now for the short sword, the claymore of Holy Scripture, to stab and cut, near and now. No sling and stone will avail us here, but we must take the sword. You have to slay your foe or your foe will slay you. It is with us Christians as it was with the Highlanders in battle when their leader called out to them, "Lads, there they are! If you dinna kill them they will kill you." There is no room for peace. It is war to the knife, not only now, but to life's end.

The sword is necessary for attack. I have reminded you several times already that it will not suffice for the Christian to guard against sin and ward off temptation from himself; he has to assail the powers of evil. In our case, the best method of defense is an attack. I have heard of one who would bring an action in law to gain his ends for he thought this better than being the defendant. That may be matter of question; but in war it is often safer to assail than defend. Carry the warfare into the enemy's territory. Be trying to win from the adversary, and he will not win so much from you. Do not merely be sober yourselves, but attack drunkenness. Do not be content with being free from superstition yourself, but expose it wherever it appears.

Do not merely be devout when you feel obliged to be so, but pray for the growth of the kingdom; pray always. Do not merely say, "I will keep Satan out of my family by bringing up my children aright," but go to the Sunday school, and teach other children, and so carry the war over the border. God forbid that we should ever go to war as a nation! But if we were at war with some nation on the continent, I should certainly say, "Let the continentals have the battles on their own ground; we do not want a campaign over here." It is wise to keep the war in the enemy's own regions. If we have fought the devil more in the world, he might never have been able to invade the church so terribly as he has done. Attack with the sword, for it is your calling, and thus will you best defend yourself.

We need the sword for real fighting. Do you think that you can dream yourselves into heaven? Or ride there in the chariot of ease? Or fly on the wings of brass music? You make a great mistake if you so imagine. A real war is raging, your opponents are in deadly earnest, and you must take your sword.

And, further, *we need this sword, this sword of the Spirit, which is the Word of God.* We say with David, "There is none like that; give it me." It has wrought such wonders that we prefer it to all others. No other will match the enemy's weapon. If we fight the devil with human reason, the first time our wooden sword comes in contact with a Satanic temptation it will be cut in pieces. If you do not wield a true Jerusalem blade, you are in grave peril; your weapon will break off at the hilt, and where will you be? Standing defenseless, with nothing but the handle of a broken sword in your hand, you will be the object of your adversary's ridicule. You must have this sword, for not other will penetrate the foe, and no other will last out the battle.

After twenty years, what has become of the pious resolutions of your youth? What is the staying power of your consecration made in the hour of enthusiasm? Alas, how little trust can be placed in it! What would become of us after thirty years of fighting, if we had not the Word of God to rely upon? The Word of the Lord endures forever; but nothing else does. We may do well in early days, but we shall fail in old age if we have not eternal verities to fall back upon.

I can commend this sword to all, although we are so

varied in character. This sword suits every hand. Youth or age may alike use this weapon. These dear girls from the Orphanage, and yonder lads from the Bible class, may fight the battle of their youth with the Word of God for Holy Scripture may impress and guide our freshest life. You who have grown gray, you who have passed seventy or eighty, you will value the Bible more than ever, and you will find that this sword is the best for veteran warriors. Young men and young women, here is a sword suited for all of you, and well does it become the hand of the feeblest and the gentlest. The Holy Spirit has in the sacred Word prepared an implement of warfare suited for great minds and small, for the cultured and the uneducated. A wonderful sword this is, which, in the hand of faith, reveals an adaptation marvelous to the last degree.

Whatever others may say, it is sufficient for us that this is the regulation sword. A soldier is not left to choose his own equipment; he must carry such arms as his sovereign appoints. This is the regulation sword in Christ's army. The sword of the Spirit, which is the Word of God, is what you are bidden to take; and if you in willfulness resolve to exchange it for another, you commit an act of rebellion, and you make the change at your own risk and peril. Come, then, let us each one take the Word of God, and carry it nearer our hearts than ever; for such is the word of command, "Take the sword of the Spirit, which is the word of God."

Now, see what we are told to do. We need *a* sword; we need *this* sword; *we are to take this sword.* Note that we are not told that we may lay it down. The demand to take the sword is continuous, and there is no hint of its being suspended. There is a time, of course, when the soldier of her Majesty may remove his sword from his side, and put off his regimentals; there is never such a time with a Christian. One might have thought, from what we have seen of late, that orders had come from headquarters that the soldiers were to lay down the sword of the Spirit, the Word of God, and take to lighter weapons. Entertainments, amusements, farces, and sing-song are now used to do what the gospel has failed to achieve! Is it not sadly so? Well, if any will try these silly toys, I can only say that they have no command from their Lord to warrant them in their proceedings. Take all these things and see what they will do; but you make the trial at your own risk, and on your own heads the result of failure will fall.

The standing orders are to take the sword of the Spirit, and no new regulation has ever been issued by the great Captain of salvation. From the days of Paul till now, the word stands, "Take the sword of the Spirit." All other things will surely fail, and hence the one sole abiding command is, "Take the sword of the Spirit." We are not told to hand up this sword for exhibition. Certain people have a handsomely bound Bible to lay upon the table of the best room; and a fine ornament it is. A Family Bible is a treasure. But I pray you do not let your love of the Bible end there. With a soldier in war, a sword is not meant to be hung up in the tent, nor even to be flourished in the air; but it is issued to be *used.*

Nor are we to push this sword into a sheath, as many do who take the Bible, and add so much of criticism, or of their own opinion to it, that its edge is not felt. Many use their low opinion of inspiration as a scabbard into which they push the Bible down. Their vast knowledge makes a beautiful scabbard, and they push down the sword, saying, "Keep still there! O sword of the Lord, rest and quiet!" After we have preached our heart out, and men have felt the power of it, they make a desperate effort to imprison the Word in their unbelieving theory or in their worldliness. They hold down the Word all the week with a firm hand for fear its edge or point should wound them. It is the scabbard of culture, or philosophy, or of progress, and in this they shut up the living Word of God as in a coffin.

We are not to bury the Word under other matters; but we are to take it as a sword which means, as I understand it, first, *believe it.* Believe every portion of it; believe it with a true and real faith, not with a mere credal faith, which says, "This is the orthodox thing." Believe it as a matter of fact for every day, affecting your life. Believe it. And when you have believed it, then *study it.* Oh, for a closer study of the Word of God! Are there not some of you who have never even heard or read all that the Lord has said? Are there not passages of the Bible which have never been read by you? It is a melancholy fact that there should be even a line of the sacred Scriptures which has once come under your eye. Do read the Bible right through, from beginning to end. Begin tomorrow; nay, begin today, and go steadily through the whole of the sacred books with prayer and meditation. Never let it be suspected by you that God has recorded truths in His Word which you have never even once read.

Study the Word, and work out its meaning. Go deep into the spirit of inspiration. He gets most gold who digs the deepest in this mine. They used to say of certain mines in Cornwall that the deeper you went the richer was the ore; assuredly is it so with the mines of inspired Scripture. The deeper you go under the Spirit's guidance the larger is the reward for your toil. Take the sword with the grip of sincere faith; hold it fast by a fuller knowledge, and then exercise yourself daily in its use. The sword is to be taken for earnest fight. You will not be long before occasion arises in such a world as this. You will have to parry with it, to pierce with it, to cut with it, and to kill with it. "Where shall I begin?" says one. Begin at home, and, for many a day, you will have your hands full. When you have slain all the rebels at home, and long before that, you may take a turn at those around you in the world, and in the professing church. Inside your own heart you will find a band of bandits which should be exterminated. There will always be need to keep the sword going within your own territory.

End this civil war before you go into foreign parts. When the war within the city of Mansoul has been victoriously carried through, besiege the heart of your friend, your child, your neighbor. Behold, the world lieth in the wicked one! Errors abound, and colossal systems of falsehood still stand aloft. Men are still dragged down by the arch-deceiver. Surely, we feel our swords flying out of their sheaths when we think of the millions who are being ruined by sin and error. Oh, for a mighty onslaught upon the powers of darkness!

Once more, *we are to take this sword with a purpose.* We are to use it that we may be able to stand and to withstand. If you want to stand, draw the sword, and smite your doubts. How fiercely unbelief assails! Here comes a doubt as to your election. Pierce it through with the Word. Perhaps there comes a doubt as to the precious blood. Cleave it from head to foot with the assurance of the Word that the blood of Jesus cleanseth us from all sin. Here comes another doubt, and yet another. As quick as arm can move, drive texts of Scripture through every new fallacy, every new denial of truth, and spit the whole of them upon the rapier of the Word. It will be for your good to kill these doubts outright. Do not play with them, but fight them in real earnest. You will find that temptations also will come in hordes. Meet them with the precepts of sacred Writ, and slay even the desire of evil by the Spirit's application of the Holy Word. The washing of water by the Word is a glorious cleanser. Discouragements will arise like mists of the morning. Oh, that God's Word may shine them away with the beams of the promises! You afflictions multiply, and you will never be able to overcome impatience and distrust except by the infallible Word of God. You can bear trial, and bear it patiently, if you use this weapon to kill anxiety. You will "stand fast in the evil day," and having done all, you will still stand, if this sword be in your hand.

You have not only to stand fast yourselves, but *you have to win souls for Christ.* Do not try to conquer sin in others, or capture a heart for Jesus, except with the sword of the Spirit. How the devil laughs when we try to make converts apart from Holy Scripture and the Holy Spirit! He laughs, I say, for he derides our folly. What can you do, you children, playing with your little wooden sword—what can you do against men covered from head to foot with the steel mail of the habit of sin? Sunday school teachers, teach your children more and more the pure Word of God; and preachers, do not try to be original, but be content to take of the things of Christ, and show them to the people for that is what the Holy Spirit Himself does; and you will be wise to use His method and His sword. No sinner around you will be saved except by the knowledge of the great truths contained in the Word of God. No man will ever be brought to repentance, to faith, and to life in Christ, apart from the constant application of the truth through the Spirit. I hear great shouting, great noises everywhere, about great things that are going to be done. Let us see them. The whole is going to be embraced within the church; so they say. I fear the world will not be much the better for inclusion in such a church. Big boasters should heed the word of the wise man, "Let not him that girdeth on his harness boast himself as he that putteth it off." If the champion goeth forth with any other sword than the Word of God, he had better not boast at all; for he will come back with his sword broken, his shield cast away, and himself grimy with dishonor. Defeat awaits that man who forsakes the Word of the Lord.

I have done when I have asked you to remember that the text is in the present tense: *Take unto you the sword of the Spirit even now.* What varieties of people there are here. Believers have come hither in all sorts of perils; let them each one take the sword of the Spirit, and they will overcome every foe. Here, too, are seekers who wish to be Christians; but they cannot compass it. What is the matter? "Oh," says one, "I have been in the habit of sinning, and the habit is very strong upon me." Fight sinful habits with the Word of God as the sword of the Spirit; so only will you conquer your evil self. Find a text of Scripture that will cleave your sin down to the bone, or stab it to the heart. "Alas! Satan tempts me horribly," cries one; "I have been lately assailed in many ways." Have you? You are not the first. Our divine Lord in the wilderness was tempted of the devil. He might have fought Satan with a thousand weapons; but He chose to defeat him with this one only. He said, "It is written; it is written; it is written." He pricked the foeman so sorely with this sharp point, that the arch-adversary thought to try the same sword; and he also began to say, "It is written." But he cut himself with this sword for he did not quote the passages correctly, nor give the whole of them; and the Master soon found the way to knock aside his sword and wound him still more. Follow your Lord's example.

"Oh, but," says one, "I am so low in spirits." Very well; fight lowness of spirits with the Word of God. "The doctor recommended me," says one, "to take a little spirits to raise my spirits." Those doctors are always having this sin laid to their charge. I am not so sure that they are not often maligned. You like the dose, and that is why you take it. Try the Word of God for lowness of spirits, and you will have found a sure remedy. I find, if I can lay a promise under my tongue, like a sweet lozenge, and keep it in my mouth or mind all the day long, I am happy enough. If I cannot find a Scripture to comfort me, then my inward troubles are multiplied. Fight despondency and despair with the sword of the Spirit.

I cannot tell what your particular difficulty may be at this moment; but I give you this direction for all holy warfare—"Take the sword of the Spirit, which is the word of God." You must overcome every enemy; and this weapon is all you need. If you, my hearer, would overcome sin and conquer unbelief, take such a word as this, "Look unto me, and be ye saved, all the ends of the earth"; and as you look you shall be saved, and doubt shall die, and sin be slain. God grant you His Spirit's aid, for Christ's sake!

NOTES

Satanic Hindrances

Charles Haddon Spurgeon (1834-1892) is undoubtedly the most famous minister of modern times. Converted in 1850, he united with the Baptists and soon began to preach in various places. He became pastor of the Baptist church in Waterbeach in 1851, and three years later he was called to the decaying Park Street Church, London. Within a short time, the work began to prosper, a new church was built and dedicated in 1861, and Spurgeon became London's most popular preacher. In 1855, he began to publish his sermons weekly; and today they make up the fifty-seven volumes of *The Metropolitan Pulpit.* He founded a pastor's college and several orphanages.

This sermon is taken from volume II of *The Metropolitan Tabernacle Pulpit,* pp. 601-612. It was preached at The Tabernacle on Sunday morning, October 29, 1865.

Charles Haddon Spurgeon

8

SATANIC HINDRANCES

Satan hindered us   (1 Thessalonians 2:18).

PAUL, AND SILAS, AND TIMOTHY, were very desirous to visit the Church at Thessalonica, but they were unable to do so for the singular reason announced in the text, namely, "Satan hindered us." *It was not from want of will,* for they had a very great attachment to the Thessalonian brethren, and they longed to look them in the face again. They said of the Thessalonians, "We give thanks to God always for you all, your work of faith, and labor of love, and patience of hope in our Lord Jesus Christ, in the sight of God and our Father." Their will was overruled as to visiting the Church together, but being anxious for its welfare, they sent Timothy alone to minister for a time in its midst. It was not want of will which hindered them, but want of power.

They were not prevented by God's special providence. We find on certain occasions that Paul was not allowed to go precisely where his heart would have led him. "They assayed to go into Bithynia: but the Spirit suffered them not." "They were forbidden of the Holy Spirit to preach the word in Asia," but their course was directed toward Troas that they might preach in Europe the unsearchable riches of Christ. They could not, however, trace their absence from Thessalonica to any divine interposition; it appeared to them to proceed from the great adversary: "Satan hindered them."

How Satan did so it would be useless to affirm dogmatically, but we may form a reasonable conjecture. I find in the margin of my pulpit Bible by Bagster, this note, which may probably be correct. "Satan hindered Paul by raising such a storm of persecution against him at Berea, and other places, that it was deemed prudent to delay his visit till the storm was somewhat allayed." Yet I can hardly allow this to have

121

been the only hindrance, for Paul was very courageous, and having a strong desire to visit Thessalonica, no fear of opposition would have kept him away. He did not shun the hottest part of the battle, but like a truly valiant champion, delighted most to be found in the thick of his foes.

Possibly the antagonism of the various philosophers whom he met with at Athens, and the heresies at Corinth, from which it seems that this epistle was written, may have called for his presence on the scene of action. He felt that he could not leave struggling churches to their enemies; he must contend with the grievous wolves, and unmask the evil ones who wore the garb of angels of light. Satan had moved the enemies of the truth to industrious opposition, and thus the apostle and his companions were hindered from going to Thessalonica.

Or it may be that Satan had excited dissensions and discords in the churches which Paul was visiting, and therefore he was obliged to stop first in one and then in another to settle their differences; to bring to bear the weight of his own spiritual influence upon the various divided sections of the church to restore them to unity. Well, whether persecution, or philosophic heresy, or the divisions of the church, were the outward instruments we cannot tell, but Satan was assuredly the prime mover.

You will perhaps wonder why the devil should care so much about Paul and his whereabouts. Why should he take so much interest in keeping these three men from that particular church? This leads us to observe that wonderful importance is attached to the action of Christian ministers. Here is the master of all evil, the prince of the power of the air, intently watching the journeying of three humble men; and apparently far more concerned about their movements than about the doings of Nero or Tiberius. These despised heralds of mercy were his most dreaded foes; they preached that name which makes hell tremble; they declared that righteousness against which Satanic hate always vents itself with its utmost power. With malicious glance the archenemy watched their daily path, and with cunning hand hindered them at all points.

It strikes us that Satan was desirous to keep these apostolic men from the Church of Thessalonica because the church was young and weak, and he thought that if it was not fostered and succored by the preaching and presence of Paul he might yet slay the young child. Moreover, he has of old a fierce hatred of the preaching of the gospel, and possibly there had been no public declaration of the truth throughout Thessalonica since Paul had gone, and he was afraid lest the fire-brands of gospel truth should be again flung in among the masses, and a gracious conflagration should take place. Besides, Satan always hates Christian fellowship; it is his policy to keep Christians apart. Anything which can divide saints from one another he delights in. He attaches far more importance to godly intercourse than we do. Since union is strength, he does his best to promote separation. He would keep Paul away from these brethren who might have gladdened his heart, and whose hearts he might have cheered; he would hinder their fraternal intercourse that they might miss the strength which always flows from Christian communion and Christian sympathy.

This is not the only occasion in which Satan has hindered good men. Indeed, this has been his practice in all ages, and we have selected this one particular incident that some who are hindered by Satan may draw comfort from it, and that we may have an opportunity (if the Spirit of God shall enable us) of saying a good and forceful word to any who count it strange because this fiery trial has happened unto them.

Satan Loves to Hinder

Let us open our discourse by observing that *it has been Satan's practice of old to hinder, wherever he could, the work of God.* "Satan hindered us" is the testimony which all the saints in heaven will bear against the archenemy. This is the witness of all who have written a holy line on the historic page, or carved a consecrated name on the rock of immortality, "Satan hindered us."

In sacred writ, we find Satan interfering to hinder the completeness of *the personal character of individual saints.*

Job was perfect and upright before God, and to all appearance, would persevere in producing a finished picture of what the believer in God should be. Indeed so had he been enabled to live that the arch-fiend could find no fault with his actions, and only dared to impute wrong motives to him. He had considered Job, and he could find no mischief in him; but then he hinted, "Hast not thou made an hedge about him, and about his house, and about all that he hath on every side?" Satan sought to turn the life-blessing which Job was giving to God into a curse, and therefore he buffeted him sorely. He stripped him of all his substance. The evil messengers trod upon one another's heels, and their tidings of woe only ceased when his goods were all destroyed and his children had all perished.

The poor afflicted parent was then smitten in his bone and in his flesh, till he had to sit upon a dunghill and scrape himself with a potsherd. Even then the picture had no blot of sin upon it, the pencil was held with a steady hand by the patient one; and therefore Satan made another attempt to hinder his retaining his holy character; he excited his wife to say, "Wherefore dost thou hold fast thy integrity? Curse God, and die." This was a great and grievous hindrance to the completion of Job's marvelous career, but, glory be unto God, the man of patience not only overcame Satan, but he made him a stepping-stone to a yet greater height of illustrious virtue; for we know the patience of Job, and we would not have known it if Satan had not illuminated it with the blaze of flaming afflictions. Had not the vessel been burnt in the furnace, the bright colors had not been so fixed and abiding. The trial through which Job passed brought out the luster of his matchless endurance in submission and resignation to God.

Now, just as the enemy of old waylaid and beset the patriarch to hinder his perseverance in the fair path of excellence, so will he do with us. You may be congratulating yourself, "I have hitherto walked consistently; no man can challenge my integrity." Beware of boasting, for your virtue will yet be tried; Satan will direct his engines against that very virtue for which you are the most famous. If you have been hitherto a firm believer, your faith will before long be attacked; if up till now you have been meek as Moses, expect to be tempted to speak unadvisedly with your lips. The birds will peck at your ripest fruit, and the wild boar will dash his tusks at your choicest vines. O that we had among us more eminence of piety, more generosity of character, more fidelity of the highest aims and intentions, but alas! how often have they had to cry, "Satan hindered us!"

This is not the enemy's only business; for he is very earnest in endeavoring to hinder *the emancipation of the Lord's redeemed ones.* You know the memorable story of Moses. When the children of Israel were in captivity in Egypt, God's servant stood before their haughty oppressor with his rod in his hand and in Jehovah's name he declared, "Thus saith the Lord, Let my people go, that they may serve me." A sign was required. The rod was cast upon the ground, and it became a serpent.

At this point, Satan hindered. Jannes and Jambres withstood Moses. We read that the magicians did so with their enchantments, whether by devilish arts or by sleight of hand, we need not now inquire. In either case they did the devil service, and they did it well—for Pharaoh's heart was hardened when he saw that the magicians wrought, in appearance, the self-same miracles as Moses. Take this as a type of Satan's hindrances to the word of the Lord. Christ's servant was come forth to preach the gospel; their ministry was attended with signs and wonders. "My kingdom is shaken," said the prince of evil, "I must bestir myself"; and straightway he sent magicians to work lying signs and wonders without number. Apocryphal wonders were and are as plentiful as the frogs of Egypt. Did the apostles preach the sacrifice of Christ?—the devil's apostles preached the sacrifice of the mass. Did the saints uplift the cross?—the devil's servants upheld the crucifix. Did God's ministers speak of Jesus as the one infallible Head of the Church?—the devil's servants proclaimed the false priest of Rome as standing in the self-same place. Romanism is a most ingenious imitation of the gospel; it is the magicians "doing so with their enchantments."

If you study well the spirit and genius of the great Antichrist, you will see that its great power lies in its

being an exceedingly clever counterfeit of the gospel of
the Lord Jesus Christ. As far as tinsel could counterfeit
gold, and paste could simulate the gem, and candlelight
could rival the sun in its glory, and a drop in the bucket
could imitate the sea in its strength, it has copied God's
great masterpiece, the gospel of our Lord Jesus Christ;
and to this day, as God's servants scatter the pure gold of
truth, their worst enemies are those who utter base coin
on which they have feloniously stamped the image and
superscription of the King of Kings.

You have another case farther on its history—and all
Old Testament history is typical of what is going on around
us now. God was about to give a most wonderful system
of instruction to Israel and to the human race, by way of
type and ceremony, in the wilderness. Aaron and his sons
were selected to represent the great High Priest of our
salvation, the Lord Jesus Christ. In every garment which
they wore there was a symbolical significance; every vessel of that sanctuary in which they ministered taught a
lesson; every single act of worship, whether it were the
sprinkling of blood or the burning of incense, was made to
teach precious and important truths to the sons of men.
What a noble roll was that volume of the book which was
unfolded in the wilderness at the foot of Sinai! How God
declared Himself and the glory of the coming Messiah in
the persons of Aaron and his sons! What then? With this
Satan interfered. Moses and Aaron could say, "Satan hindered us." Korah, Dathan, and Abiram arrogantly claimed
a right to the priesthood; and on a certain day they stood
forth with brazen censers in their hands, thrusting themselves impertinently into the office which the Lord has
assigned to Aaron and to his sons. The earth opened and
swallowed them up alive—true prophecy of what shall
become of those who thrust themselves into the office of
the priesthood where none but Jesus Christ can stand.

You may see the parallel today. Christ Jesus is the
only priest who offers sacrifice of blood, and He brings
that sacrifice no more; for having once offered it, He has
perfected forever those who are set apart. "This man,
after he had offered one sacrifice for sins forever, sat down

on the right hand of God." Paul, with the strongest force of logic, proves that Christ does not offer a continual sacrifice, but that, having offered it once for all, His work is finished, and He sits down at the right hand of the Father. Now, this doctrine of a finished atonement and a completed sacrifice seemed likely to overrun the world—it was such a gracious unfolding of the divine mind that Satan could not look upon it without desiring to hinder it; and, therefore, look on every hand, and you can see Korah, Dathan, and Abiram, in those churches which are branches of Antichrist. Men to this very day call themselves "priests," and read prayers from a book. Thus the ministers of Jesus are made to cry, "Satan hindereth us."

Take another instance of Satanic hatred. When Joshua had led the tribes across the Jordan, they were to attack the various cities which God had given them for a heritage, and from Dan to Beersheba the whole land was to be theirs. After the taking of Jericho, the first contact into which they came with the heathen Canaanites ended in a disastrous defeat to the servants of God. "They fled," it is written, "before the men of Ai." Here again you hear the cry, "Satan hindered us." Joshua might have gone from city to city exterminating the nations, as they justly deserved to be, but Achan had taken of the accursed thing and hidden it in his tent, therefore no victory could be won by Israel till his theft and sacrilege had been put away. This is true of the Christian church today. We might go from victory to victory; our home mission operations might be successful, and our foreign agencies might be crowned with triumph, if it were not that we have Achans in the camp at home. When churches have no conversions, it is more than probable that hypocrites concealed among them have turned away the Lord's blessing.

You who are inconsistent, who make the profession of religion the means of getting wealth, you who unite yourselves with God's people, but at the same time covet the goodly Babylonish garment and the wedge of gold, you are those who cut the sinews of Zion's strength; you prevent the Israel of God from going forth to victory. Ah! little do we know how Satan has hindered us. We, as a church, have had much reason to thank God, but how many more might within these walls have been added to the number of this church if it had not been for the coldness of some, the indifference of others, the inconsistency of a few, and the worldliness of many more! Satan hinders us not merely by direct opposition, but by sending Achans into the midst of our camp.

I will give you one more picture. View the building of Jerusalem after it had been destroyed by the Babylonians. When Ezra and Nehemiah were found to build, the devil was sure to stir up Sanballat and Tobiah to cast down. There was never a revival of religion without a revival of the old enmity. If ever the Church of God is to be built, it will be in troublous times. When God's servants are active, Satan is not without vigilant mercenaries who seek to counteract their efforts.

The history of the Old Testament Church is a history of Satan endeavoring to hinder the work of the Lord. I am sure you will admit it has been the same since the days of the Lord Jesus Christ. When He was on earth Satan hindered Him. He dared to attack Him to His face personally; and when that failed, Pharisees, Sadducees, Herodians, and men of all sorts hindered Him. When the apostles began their ministry, Herod and the Jews sought to hinder them; and when persecution did not avail, then all sorts of heresies and schisms broke out in the Christian Church. Satan still hindered them. A very short time after the taking up of our Lord, the precious sons of Zion, comparable to fine gold, had become like earthen pitchers, the work of the hands of the potter; the glory had departed, and the luster of truth was gone, because by false doctrine, lukewarmness, and worldliness, Satan hindered them.

When the Reformation dawned, if God raised up a Luther, the devil brought out an Ignatius Loyola to hinder him. Here in England, if God had His Latimers and His Wickcliffs, the devil had his Gardiners and Bonners. When in the later reformation Whitfield and Wesley thundered like the voice of God, there were ordained reprobates found to hinder them, to hold them up to opprobrium and shame. Never, since the first hour struck in which goodness came into conflict with evil, has it ceased to be true that Satan hindered us. From all points of the compass, all along the line of battle, in the vanguard and in the rear, at the dawn of day and in the midnight, Satan hindered us. If we toil in the field, he seeks to break the ploughshare; if we build the walls, he labors to cast down the stones; if we would serve God in suffering or in conflict—everywhere Satan hinders us.

How Satan Hinders

We shall now, in the second place, *indicate many ways in which Satan has hindered us.* The prince of evil is very busy in hindering *those who are just coming to Jesus Christ.* Here he spends the main part of his skill. Some of us who know the Savior recollect the fierce conflicts which we had with Satan when we first looked to the cross and lived. Others of you are just passing through that trying season; I will address myself to you. Beloved friends, you long to be saved, but ever since you have given any attention to these eternal things you have been the victim of deep distress of mind. Do not marvel at this. This is usual, so usual as to be almost universal. I should not wonder if you are perplexed with the doctrine of election. It will be suggested to you that you are not one of the chosen of God, although your common sense will teach you that it might just as well be suggested to you that you are, since you know neither the one nor the other, nor indeed can know until you have believed in Jesus; your present business is with the precept which is revealed, not with election which is concealed. Your business is with that exhortation, "Believe on the Lord Jesus Christ, and thou shalt be saved."

It is possible that the great fighting-ground between predestination and free-will may be the dry and desert place in which your soul is wandering now. You will never find any comfort there. The wisest of men have despaired of ever solving the mystery of those two matters, and it is not at all probable that you will find peace in puzzling yourself about it. Your business is not with metaphysical difficulty, but with faith in the atonement of the Lord Jesus Christ which is simple and plain enough. It is possible that your sins now come to your remembrance, and though once you thought little enough of them, now it is hinted to you by Satanic malice that they are too great to be pardoned; to which, I pray you, give the lie, by telling Satan this truth, that "All manner of sin and blasphemy shall be forgiven unto men."

It is very likely that the sin against the Holy Spirit much troubles you. You read that whosoever shall speak a word against the Holy Spirit, it shall never be forgiven him. In this, too, you may be greatly tried; and I wonder not that you are, for this is a most painfully difficult subject. One fact may cheer you—if you repent of your sins, you have not committed the unpardonable offense since that sin necessitates hardness of heart forever; and so long as a man has any tenderness of conscience, and any softness of spirit, he has not so renounced the Holy Spirit as to have lost His presence. It may be that you are the victim of blasphemous thoughts. At this be not astonished, for there are some of us who delight in holiness and are pure in heart, who nevertheless, have been at times sorely tried with thoughts which were never born in our hearts, but which were injected into them—suggestions born in hell, not in our spirits—to be hated, and to be loathed, but cast into our minds that they might hinder and trouble us.

Now, though Satan may hinder you as he did the child who was brought to Jesus of whom we read that as he was "a coming, the devil threw him down and tare him," yet do thou come notwithstanding; for though seven devils were in him, Jesus would not cast the coming sinner out. Even though you should feel a conviction that the unpardonable sin has fallen to your lot, yet dare to trust in Jesus; and, if you do that, I warrant there shall be a joy and a peace in believing which shall overcome him of whom we read, that he hath "hindered us."

But I must not stop long on any one point where there are so many. Satan is sure to hinder Christians *when they are earnest in prayer.* Have you not frequently found when you have been most earnest in supplication, that something or other will start across your mind to make you cease from the exercise? It appears to me that we shake the tree and no fruit drops from it; and just when one more shake would bring down the luscious fruit, the devil touches us on the shoulder and tells us it is time to be gone, and so we miss the blessing we might have attained. I mean that just when prayer would be the most successful we are tempted to abstain from it. When my spirit has sometimes laid hold upon the angel, I have been painfully conscious of a counterinfluence urging me to cease from such importunity and let the Lord alone, for His will would be done; or if the temptation did not come in that shape yet in some other, to cease to pray because prayer after all could not prevail. O brethren, I know if you are much in prayer you can sing Cowper's hymn—

"What various hindrances we meet
In coming to the mercy seat."

The same is true of *Christians when under the promptings of the Spirit of God, or when planning any good work.* You have been prompted sometimes to speak to such a one. "Run, speak to that young man" has been the message in your ear. You have not done it—Satan has hindered you. You have been told on a certain occasion— you do not know how (but believe me we ought to pay great respect to these inward whispers) to visit such-and- such a person and help him. You have not done it—Satan hindered you. You have been sitting down by the fire one evening reading a missionary report concerning a heathen land, or some district destitute of the truth, and you have thought "Now I have a little money which I might give to this object"; but then it has come across you that there is another way of spending it more profitably to your family— so Satan has hindered you. Or you yourself thought of doing a little in a certain district by way of preaching, and teaching, or commencing some new Ragged School, or some other form of Christian effort, but as sure as ever you began to plan it something or other arose, and Satan hindered you. If he possibly can, he will come upon God's people in those times when they are full of thought and ardor and ready for Christian effort, that he may murder their infant plans and cast these suggestions of the Holy Spirit out of their minds.

How often too has Satan hindered us when *we have*

entered into the work! In fact, we never ought to expect a success unless we hear the devil making a noise. I have taken it as a certain sign that I am doing little good when the devil is quiet. It is generally a sign that Christ's kingdom is coming when men begin to lie about you, and slander you, and the world is in an uproar, casting out your name as evil. Oh! those blessed tempests! Do not give me calm weather when the air is still and heavy, and when lethargy is creeping over one's spirit. Lord, send a hurricane, give us a little stormy weather. When the lightning flashes and the thunder rolls, then God's servants know that the Lord is abroad and that His right hand is no longer in His bosom, that the moral atmosphere will get clear, that God's kingdom will come, and His will be done on earth, even as it is in heaven.

"Peace, peace, peace," that is the flap of the dragon's wings; the stern voice which proclaims perpetual war is the voice of the Captain of our salvation. You say, how is this? "Think not that I am come to send peace on earth: I came not to send peace, but a sword. For I am come to set a man at variance against his father, and the daughter against her mother, and the daughter-in-law against her mother-in-law. And a man's foes shall be they of his own household." Peace, physical, Christ does make; there is to be no strife with the fist, no blow with the sword; but peace, moral, and peace, spiritual, can never be in this world where Jesus Christ is so long as error is there.

But, you know, beloved, that you cannot do any good thing but what the devil will be sure to hinder you. What then? Up and at him! Cowardly looks and faint counsels are not for warriors of the cross. Expect fightings and you will not be disappointed. Whitfield used to say that some divines would go from the first of January to the end of December with a perfectly whole skin; the devil never thought them worth while attacking; but, said he, let us begin to preach with all our might, and soul, and strength, the gospel of Jesus Christ, and men will soon put a fool's cap on our heads, and begin laughing at us, and ridiculing us, but if so, so much the better. We are not alarmed because Satan hinders us.

Nor will he only hinder us in working; he will hinder us

in seeking to unite with one another. We are about to make an effort, as Christian churches in London, to come closer together, and I am happy to find indications of success; but I should not wonder but what Satan will hinder us, and I would ask your prayers that Satan may be put rout in this matter, and that the union of our churches may be accomplished. As a church ourselves, we have walked together in peace for a long time, but I should not marvel if Satan should try to thrust in the cloven foot to hinder our walking in love, and peace, and unity.

Satan will hinder us *in our communion with Jesus Christ.* When at His table we say to ourselves, "I shall have a sweet moment now," but just then vanity intrudes. Like Abraham, you offer the sacrifice, but the unclean birds come down upon it, and you have need to drive them away. "Satan hindered us." He is not omnipresent, but by his numerous servants he works in all kinds of places, and manages to distract the saints when they would serve the Lord.

How to See Satan

In the third place *there are two or three rules by which these hindrances may be detected as Satanic.* I think I heard somebody saying to himself this morning, "Yes, I should have risen in the world, and have been a man of money now if it had not been that Satan hindered me." Do not you believe it, dear friend. I do not believe that Satan generally hinders people from getting rich. He would just as soon that they should be rich as poor. He delights to see God's servants set upon the pinnacle of the temple for he knows the position to be dangerous. High places and God's praise do seldom well agree. If you have been hindered in growing rich, I should rather set that down to the good providence of God which would not place you where you could not have borne the temptation. "Yes," said another, "I had intended to have lived in a certain district and done good, and have not been able to go: perhaps that is the devil." Perhaps it was; perhaps it was not. God's providence will know best where to place us. We are not always choosers of our own locality, and so we are not always to conclude when we are hindered and disappointed in our own intentions that Satan has done it, for it may very often be the good providence of God.

But how may I tell when Satan hinders me? I think you may tell thus: first, *by the object*. Satan's object in hindering us is to prevent our glorifying God. If anything has happened to you which has prevented your growing holy, useful, humble, and sanctified, then you may trace that to Satan. If the distinct object of the interference to the general current of your life has been that you may be turned from sin into righteousness, then from the object you may guess that God does sometimes put apparent hindrances in the way of His own people, even in reference to their usefulness and growth in grace, but then His object is still to be considered—it is to try His saints and so to strengthen them while the object of Satan is to turn them out of the right road and make them take the crooked way.

You may tell the suggestions of Satan, again, by *the method* in which they come: God employs good motives, Satan, bad ones. If that which has turned you away from your object has been a bad thought, a bad doctrine, bad teaching, a bad motive—that never came from God, that must be from Satan.

Again, you may tell them from *their nature*. Whenever an impediment to usefulness is pleasing, gratifying to you, consider that it came from Satan. Satan never brushes the feathers of his birds the wrong way; he generally deals with us according to our tastes and likings. He flavors his bait to his fish. He knows exactly how to deal with each man and to put that motive which will fall in with the suggestions of poor carnal nature. Now, if the difficulty in your way is rather contrary to yourself, then it comes from God; but if that which now is a hindrance brings you gain, or pleasure, or emolument in any way, rest assured it came from Satan.

We can tell the suggestions of Satan, once more, *by their season*. Hindrances to prayer, for instance, if they are Satanic, come *out of the natural course and relation of human thoughts*. It is a law of mental science that one thought suggests another, and the next the next, and so on, as the links of a chain draw one another. But Satanic temptations do not come in the regular order of thinking; they dash upon the mind unawares. My soul is in prayer; it would be unnatural that I should then blaspheme, yet then the blasphemy comes; therefore it is clearly Satanic, and not from my own mind. If I am set upon doing my Master's will and presently a recreant thought assails me, that, being apart from the natural run of my mind and thoughts, may be at once ejected as not being mine, and may be set down to the account of the devil who is the true father of it.

By these means I think we may tell when Satan hinders, and when it is our own heart, or when it is of God. We ought carefully to watch that we do not put the saddle on the wrong horse. Do not blame the devil when it is yourself, and on the other hand, when the Lord puts a bar in your way, do not say, "That is Satan," and so go against the providence of God. It may be difficult at times to see the way of duty, but if you go to the throne of God in prayer you will soon discover it. "Bring hither the ephod," said David, when he was in difficulty. Say you the same? Go you to the great High Priest, whose business it is to give forth the oracle! Lo, upon His breast hangs the Urim and Thummim, and you shall from him find direction in every time of difficulty and dilemma.

What to Do about It

Supposing that we have ascertained that hindrances in our way really come from Satan, *what then?*

I have but one piece of advice, and that is, *go on,* hindrance or no hindrance, in the path of duty as God the Holy Spirit enables you. If Satan hinders you, I have already hinted that this *opposition should cheer you.* "I did not expect," said a Christian minister, "to be easy in this particular pastorate, or else I would not have come here; for I always count it," said he, "to be my duty to show the devil that I am his enemy, and if I do that, I expect that he will show me that he is mine." If you are now opposed and you can trace that opposition distinctly to Satan, congratulate yourself upon it, do not sit down and fret. Why, it is a great thing that a poor creature like you can actually vex the great prince of darkness and win his hate. It makes the race of man the more noble that it comes in conflict with a race of spirits and stands foot to foot even with the prince of darkness himself. It is a dreadful thing, doubtless, that you should be hindered by such an adversary, but it is most hopeful, for if he were your friend you might have cause to fear indeed. Stand out against him, because *you have now an opportunity of making a greater gain than you could have made had he been quiet.* You could never have had a victory over him if you had not engaged in conflict with him. The poor saint would go on his inglorious way to heaven if he were unmolested, but being molested, every step of his pathway becomes glorious. Our position today is like that described by Bunyan, when from the top of the palace the song was heard—

"Come in, come in,
Eternal glory thou shalt win."

Now merely to ascend the stairs of the palace, though safe work, would not have been very ennobling; but when the foemen crowded round the door, and blocked up every stair, and the hero came to the man with the ink-horn who sat before the door and said, "Write my name down, sir"; then to get from the lowest step to the top where the bright ones were singing, every inch was glorious. If devils did not oppose my path from earth to heaven, I might travel joyously, peacefully, safely, but certainly without renown; but now, when every step is contested in winning our pathway to glory, every single step is covered with immortal fame.

Be in earnest against these hindrances when you consider, again, *what you lose if you do not resist him and overcome him.* To allow Satan to overcome me would be eternal ruin to my soul. Certainly it would forever blast all hopes of my usefulness. If I retreat and turn my back in the day of battle, what will the rest of God's servants say? What shouts of derision will ring over the battlefield! How will the banner of the covenant be trailed in the mire! Why, we must not, we dare not, play the coward; we dare not give way to the insinuation of Satan and turn from the Master, for the defeat were then too dreadful to be endured. Beloved, let me feed your courage with the recollection that *your Lord and Master has overcome.* See him there before you. He of the thorn-crown has fought the enemy and broken his head—Satan has been completely worsted by the Captain of your salvation; and that victory was representative—He fought and won it for you. You have to contend with a defeated foe, and one who knows and feels his disgrace; and though he may fight with desperation, yet he fights not with true courage for he is hopeless of ultimate victory. Strike, then, for Christ has smitten him. Down with him, for Jesus has had him under His foot. The Captain has triumphed before you.

Lastly, remember that *you have a promise* to make you gird up your loins and play the man this day. "Resist the devil, and he shall flee from you." Christian minister, do not resign; do not think of sending your resignation because the church is divided and because the enemy is making progress. Resist the devil. Flee not, but make him flee. Christian young men, you who have begun to preach in the street or visit from house to house, though Satan hinders you very much I pray you now redouble your efforts. It is because Satan hinders you very much I pray you now redouble your efforts; it is because Satan is afraid of you that he resists you because he would rob you of the great blessing which is now descending on your head. Resist him and stand fast.

Christian pleading in prayer, do not declare your hold upon the covenant angel now; for not that Satan hinders you, it is because the blessing is descending. You who are seeking Christ, close not those eyes, turn not away your face from Calvary's streaming tree. Now that Satan hinders you, it is because the night is almost over, and the day-star begins to shine. You who are most molested, most sorrowfully tried, most borne down, yours is the brighter hope! Be now courageous; play the man for God, for Christ, for your own soul. The day shall come when you with your Master will ride triumphant through the streets of the New Jerusalem, sin, death, and hell, captive at your chariot wheels, and you with your Lord crowned as victor, having overcome through the blood of the Lamb.

The Battle for Man's Soul

Clarence Edward Noble Macartney (1879-1957)
ministered in Paterson, New Jersey, and Philadelphia,
Pennsylvania, before assuming the influential pastorate
of First Presbyterian Church, Pittsburgh, where he
ministered for twenty-seven years. His preaching especially
attracted men, not only to the Sunday services but also to
his popular Tuesday noon luncheons. He was gifted in
dealing with Bible biographies, and, in this respect, has
well been called "the American Alexander Whyte." Much
of his preaching was topical-textual, but it was always
biblical, doctrinal and practical. Perhaps his most famous
sermon is "Come Before Winter."

The sermon I have selected is taken from *Strange Texts
But Grand Truths,* published in 1953 by Abingdon Press,
New York and Nashville.

Clarence Edward Noble Macartney

9

THE BATTLE FOR MAN'S SOUL

"Michael the archangel, when contending with the devil he disputed about the body of Moses . . ." (Jude 9).

WHEN CHARLES SPURGEON was once being shown through the library of Trinity College, Cambridge, he stopped to admire a bust of Byron. The librarian said to him, "Stand here, sir, and look at it."

Spurgeon took the position indicated and, looking upon the bust, remarked, "What an intellectual countenance! What a grand genius!"

"Come, now," said the librarian, "and look at it from this side."

Spurgeon changed his position and, looking on the statue from that viewpoint, exclaimed, "What a demon! There stands a man who could defy the Deity." He asked the librarian if the sculptor had secured this effect designedly.

"Yes," he replied, "he wished to picture the two characters, the two persons—the great, the grand, the almost supergenius that he possessed; and yet the enormous mass of sin that was in his soul."

Strange, and in many ways forbidding, is this brief one-chapter book of Jude. As scowling gargoyles look menacingly down upon him who enters one of the old cathedrals, so this mysterious book is like a gargoyle at the golden gate which opens into the glorious cathedral of the Apocalypse of John, with its grand harmonies, its voices like the sound of many waters, its sea of glass mingled with fire, and its great white throne. Nowhere else in the Bible do we come upon such volcanic judgments, such overwhelming condemnation, as confront us in the Epistle of Jude. One might liken it to the enraged ocean breaking upon a rocky barrier and then retreating with sullen roar, or to a summer hurricane which sweeps over smiling fields and peaceful hamlets with the besom of destruction, or to a storm of thunder and lightning at midnight, illuminating the heavens and making the earth shake with the flash of its artillery.

What a book! Here we behold the fall of the angels and contemplate their doom as, without a Redeemer, they await, reserved in everlasting chains in darkness, the judgment of the great day. Here burn the flames of Sodom and Gomorrah, whose citizens were consumed for their unnatural crimes. Here Cain goes guiltily out from the presence of the Lord with a brand upon his brow, and here the Judge of all the earth comes in the clouds with ten thousand of his saints to execute judgment upon all that are ungodly. All that is tragic and terrible in the history of revelation and in the destiny of the universe is set forth in forbidding array in this brief but tremendous epistle.

The letter is a blast on the trumpet against the evil and the evil men which were threatening the Church. These are enemies of "the faith which was once delivered unto the saints." False in their doctrine, they are corrupt and unspeakable in their morals. To the exhortations and warnings of the Church they return scoffing and irreverent answers. To describe their unbounded license and arrogance, the inspired writer declares that they speak evil of dignities and rail at the truth; whereas even Michael, the archangel, when in dispute with the devil over the body of Moses, did not bring against him a railing accusation, but said, "The Lord rebuke thee." Michael's reserve was perhaps a tribute to the former state of Satan when he was still an unfallen spirit of God. Although Satan is now fallen and in rebellion against God, the great angel Michael, once his comrade before God's throne, remembers Satan's former estate and pays tribute to it. In contrast with his attitude toward the prince of the kingdom of wickedness, these evil men, against whom this epistle is directed, dare to treat with scorn and contempt the acknowledged teachers and apostles of the Church of Christ.

Before we come to our main proposition, there is a by-product of truth in this reference, and that is, that the friends and advocates of the truth do not need to depend upon abuse or rash anger in their encounter with the teachers and representatives of error. The truth needs no such weapons for its defense. Better the calm dignity and confidence of Michael, who said to the devil, "The Lord rebuke thee." It is well to remember that, while it is our duty to expose and denounce and condemn error, the pronouncement of judgment belongs not to man but to God.

Of this strange encounter between a fallen and an unfallen prince of heaven we have no record save this brief and cryptic allusion. As for the body of Moses, all we are told is that, having viewed the promised Land in the distance, Moses died and was buried "in the land of Moab, over against Beth-peor," and "no man knoweth of his sepulcher unto this day." In his poem, "The Burial of Moses," Cecil Frances Alexander says:

> By Nebo's lonely mountain,
> On this side Jordan's wave,
> In a vale in the land of Moab
> There lies a lonely grave;
> And no man knows that sepulcher
> And no man saw it e'er;
> For the angels of God upturn'd the sod
> And laid the dead man there.

The Conflict of Good and Evil in the World

Why should Michael and the devil dispute over the body of Moses? Why did the devil want it anyway? Some have conjectured that the language of the epistle here is figurative, and that by the body of Moses is meant the Jewish church, just as we call the Christian church the "body of Christ." Again, it has been suggested that the devil wanted to prevent the secret burial of Moses, so that his tomb might become a place of worship for the children of Israel and thus lead them into idolatry. But all this is mere surmise. Certainly the author refers to the incident as a bit of Hebrew history, or tradition, with which his readers were thoroughly familiar. We shall waste no time in the discussion of the possible historical background, but come at once to the truth for which it is a remarkable and striking setting and illustration; namely, the ceaseless struggle between good and evil in the heart of man for the dominion of the world. As the body of Moses was the subject and object of a dispute between the great archangel and the fallen prince of heaven, so the soul of man is a battleground where clash the powers of light and darkness, good and evil, Michael and the devil, heaven and hell.

The fact of this conflict is the key to human nature and human history. At the very beginning, after the fall of man, the history of the world was made the judgment of the world when God said, "I will put enmity between thee and the woman, and between thy seed and her seed." That hatred and enmity implanted at the beginning is mutual, implacable, and everlasting. The first view we have of man shows him standing on a battlefield. He is addressed by two principles of conduct—God said; the tempter said. All the struggles of history, the battles between freedom and tyranny, good government and bad government, religion and anarchy, purity and licentiousness, are but echoes of this struggle on the battlefield of man's own heart.

It is this conflict in which good causes and good works become infected with the cancer of evil. As Faber put it in his famous hymn,

> Ill masters good, good seems to change
> To ill with greatest ease;
> And, worst of all, the good with good
> Is at cross purposes.

How often we see this! The government which has been set up for man's protection and happiness sometimes becomes such an enemy of man that the best thing that can happen is its destruction. Science and education are a double-edged sword and can be turned, and have been turned, against the welfare of mankind; and what is more evident than the way in which religion has been invaded by superstition, worldliness, and corruption, so that wherever man builds a church, the devil builds a chapel? Wherever the spirit of mankind moves out with banners and trumpets on the march of progress, there marches ever on its flank the army of the powers of evil. It is this which explains the corruption of the good, and the malignity and persistence, the revival of evil in the world.

Paul struck the true and grand note when he said, exhorting the Christian disciples to courage and steadfastness in their battle with temptation and evil, that we "wrestle not against flesh and blood, but against principalities, against powers, against the rulers of the darkness of this world." Our battle is not with evil institutions, such as slavery, or the liquor evil; but with something deeper, darker, more potent, and invisible. You may destroy and overthrow a bad government; you may outlaw a wicked business or institution; but you have not killed the evil principle which animated the body in which it was for a time incarnated. We do not believe in the reincarnation of souls, but we certainly do believe in the reincarnation of evil in the world.

In *The Four Horsemen of the Apocalypse*, a book widely read during World War I, the young friend of the Russian thinker and prophet was jubilant because he thought he saw the downfall of the enemies of righteousness and the imminent overthrow of all the confederated forces of darkness and sin in the world. But the Russian prophet calmed his enthusiasm by his sad but true observation, borrowed from another great vision of the Apocalypse, the beast which emerged out of the abyss with his deadly wound healed: "No; the beast does not die. He is the eternal companion of man. He hides, spouting blood for sixty or a hundred years; but eventually he reappears."

What Jude does for us, then, in this strange book of his is to roll back, as it were, the cu ain of our horizon and permit us a momentary glimpse of the extent and range of this battle between good and evil. Its territory is as vast as the universe; its duration as long as time; its theater, the visible and the invisible worlds.

The fact of this struggle helps us to understand what is going on in the world, and with such an understanding we shall not be cast down or dismayed when we see evil, routed and vanquished in one form, returning in some new institution, and sometimes in a much worse form, just as the evicted devil of our Lord's parable, returning to his house, brought with him seven spirits worse than himself.

The Conflict in Our Soul

But, in a more personal aspect, this truth is instructive and helpful for us in our own lives. If we are sometimes a mystery to ourselves, as, no doubt, we often are to others, this is the secret and explanation of it. Victor Hugo in one of his poems wrote, "I feel two worlds struggling within me." I remember seeing once a sculpture by Carpenter which illustrated this saying. Out of a central block of marble emerge two persons, or personalities; the one, intellectual, refined, spiritual, desperately struggling to get free; the other, of the earth, earthy, animal, sensual, cruel. There in the sculptor's thought and creation is expressed what goes on beneath every human breast. Over and over again the master artists of the Bible permit us to view such a sculpture.

In beautiful language Balaam salutes the future of Israel and longs for the death of the righteous, while coveting the gold which he could have as a reward for cursing them. Judas hears the word of Christ, "Follow me," and follows Him, but only to betray Him for thirty pieces of silver; and yet, after he has betrayed Him, Judas is so stricken with remorse that he goes out and hangs himself. Pilate at once recognizes Jesus as a just man and strives to save himself from the guilt of crucifying Him; but when he hears someone shout, "Thou art not Caesar's friend," for the sake of his high place and office Pilate hands Christ over to be crucified. Peter avows that he will never forsake Christ, and in the Garden of Gethsemane he seems to make good that vow when he fearlessly draws his sword and cuts off the ear of the assailant of his Lord. Yet, before the night has passed, he has denied with an oath that he ever knew him.

Men have sometimes discussed the question of whether, when Paul spoke of the fierce conflict that was going on within his breast—the war between the law of the mind and the law of sin—he was referring to the struggles of a regenerate or an unregenerate man, the natural or the Christian man. Is it autobiographical? Or, when Paul says "I" here, does he mean unregenerate human nature? However that may be, there is no doubt that Paul's description of the struggle that went on in his breast is one which fits us all. We are born on a battlefield, and from that warfare "there is no discharge."

When we enter upon the Christian life, we are not set free from that conflict. To imagine so would be like telling a soldier who has enlisted in a regiment for a war that now, having put his name down on the muster roll of the company or regiment, he can lay by his sword and dispense with his rifle. It is when we really enlist in the Christian life and on the side of Christ that the conflict becomes intense, vivid, grim. When Jesus made his appearance in the flesh as the Son of God and the Son of man, there was a furious outbreak on the part of the demons, for they recognized the threat to their kingdom in the advent of Christ. When a man really makes an effort to follow Christ, then the battle commences. "Through much tribulation," said the greatest of all veterans in this ageless war, "we must enter into the kingdom of God." There is no other path.

The remembrance of the fact that this conflict is everywhere going on is of a nature not only to humble us and warn us, but also to fill us with the spirit of prayer and sympathy for others. If we could know the burdens, handicaps, thorns in the flesh, trials, sorrows, invisible struggles, of our fellows in this world, a wave of compassion would surely sweep over us all.

Our Captain in the Battle

But whether we sympathize with one another or not, or remember our common battles and struggles as we ought to or not, there is One who does know our battle and who sympathizes with our struggles. It is He, the great Captain of our salvation. He, too, was a soldier in this war and in it received many cruel and painful wounds. Himself having suffered, Himself having fought, He is able to help you and me in our own conflict. He is not a great high priest, a distant, remote, and austere Captain who

with cold indifference observes our battle, its daily ebb
and flow, but one who fights by our side and rejoices in
our victories. Put your faith in Him. Over and over again
it has been proved that in the time of danger and peril a
whispered prayer to Him, the very thought of His Cross
and of His love, yes, the very mention of His name, has
been a refuge from evil and a very present help in the
time of trouble.

Jude is indeed a strange book, full of difficult allusions,
flashing with lightnings, and reverberating with the thun-
ders of judgment upon fallen angels and fallen men. But
that is not all there is to this book. As a stormy day
sometimes comes to a close with a beautiful sunset, so
this brief and stormy book comes to a conclusion with one
of the grandest and most precious of all the promises and
sayings of God's Word. It is this: "Now unto him that is
able to keep you from falling, and to present you faultless
before the presence of his glory with exceeding joy, to the
only wise God our Savior, be glory and majesty, dominion
and power, both now and ever. Amen" (vv. 24,25).

NOTES

Satan's Devices

John Wesley (1703-1781), along with his brother Charles, and George Whitefield, founded the Methodist movement in Britain and America. On May 24, 1738, he had his great spiritual experience in a meeting at Aldersgate Street when his "heart was strangely warmed," and he received assurance of salvation. Encouraged by Whitefield to do open-air preaching, Wesley soon was addressing thousands in spite of the fact that many churches were closed to him. The Methodist "societies" he formed became local churches that conserved the results of his evangelism. He wrote many books and preached 40,000 sermons during his long ministry.

This sermon is taken from *Works of John Wesley*, volume 6, the reprint edition of Zondervan Publishing House, Grand Rapids, Michigan.

John Wesley

10

SATAN'S DEVICES

We are not ignorant of his devices" (2 Corinthians 2:11).

1. THE DEVICES WHEREBY the subtle god of this world labors to destroy the children of God—or at least to torment whom he cannot destroy, to perplex and hinder them in running the race which is set before them—are numberless as the stars of heaven, or the sand upon the seashore. But it is of one of them only that I now propose to speak, (although exerted in various ways,) whereby he endeavors to divide the gospel against itself, and by one part of it to overthrow the other.

2. The inward kingdom of heaven, which is set up in the hearts of all that repent and believe the gospel, is no other than "righteousness, and peace, and joy in the Holy Spirit." Every babe in Christ knows we are made partakers of these the very hour that we believe in Jesus. But these are only the first fruits of His Spirit; the harvest is not yet. Although these blessings are inconceivably great, yet we trust to see greater than these. We trust to love the Lord our God, not only as we do now, with a weak, though sincere affection, but "with all our heart, with all our mind, with all our soul, and with all our strength." We look for power to "rejoice evermore, to pray without ceasing and in every thing to give thanks"; knowing, "this is the will of God in Christ Jesus concerning us."

3. We expect to be "made perfect in love"; in that which casts out all painful fear, and all desire but that of glorifying Him we love, and of loving and serving Him more and more. We look for such an increase in the experimental knowledge and love of God our Savior as will enable us always "to walk in the light as he is in the light." We believe the whole mind will be in us, "which was in Christ Jesus"; that we shall love every man so as to be ready to lay down our life for his sake; so as, by this love, to be

freed from anger, and pride, and from every unkind affection. We expect to be "cleansed from all our idols," "from all filthiness," whether "of flesh or spirit"; to be "saved from all our uncleannesses," inward or outward; to be purified "as He is pure."

4. We trust in His promise, who cannot lie, that the time will surely come, when, in every word and work, we shall do His blessed will on earth, as it is done in heaven; when all our conversation shall be seasoned with salt, all meet to minister grace to the hearers; when, whether we eat or drink, or whatever we do, it shall be done to the glory of God; when all our words and deeds shall be "in the name of the Lord Jesus, giving thanks unto God, even the Father, through Him."

5. Now this is the grand device of Satan, to destroy the first work of God in the soul, or at least to hinder its increase by our expectation of that greater work. It is therefore my present design, first, to point out the several ways whereby He endeavors this destruction; and, secondly, to observe how we may retort these fiery darts of the wicked one—how we may rise the higher by what he intends for an occasion of our falling.

I. The Ways of Satan

I shall point out the several ways whereby Satan endeavors to destroy the first work of God in the soul, or at least to hinder its increase by our expectation of that greater work. He endeavors to damp our joy in the Lord by the consideration of our own vileness, sinfulness, unworthiness; added to this, that there must be a far greater change than is yet, or we cannot see the Lord. If we knew we must remain as we are, even to the day of our death, we might possibly draw a kind of comfort, poor as it was, from that necessity. But as we know we need not remain in this state, as we are assured there is a greater change to come, and that unless sin be all done away in this life, we cannot see God in glory—that subtle adversary often damps the joy we should otherwise feel in what we have already attained, by a perverse representation of what we have not attained, and the absolute necessity of attaining it. So that we cannot rejoice in what we have, because there is more which we have not. We cannot rightly taste the goodness of God, who has done so great things for us, because there are so much greater things which, as yet, he has not done. Likewise, the deeper conviction God works in us of our present unholiness, and the more vehement desire we feel in our heart of the entire holiness He has promised, the more are we tempted to think lightly of the present gifts of God, and to undervalue what we have already received, because of what we have not received.

2. If he can prevail thus far, if he can damp our joy, he will soon attack our peace also. He will suggest, "Are you fit to see God? He is of purer eyes than to behold iniquity. How, then, can you flatter yourself, so as to imagine He beholds you with approbation? God is holy: You are unholy. What communion hath light with darkness? How is it possible that you, unclean as you are, should be in a state of acceptance with God? You see indeed the mark, the prize of your high calling; but do you not see it is afar off? How can you presume then to think that all your sins are already blotted out? How can this be, until you are brought nearer to God, until you bear more resemblance to Him?" Thus will he endeavor not only to shake your peace, but even to overturn the very foundation of it; to bring you back, by insensible degrees, to the point from whence you set out first, even to seek for justification by works, or by your own righteousness—to make something in you the ground of your acceptance, or, at least, necessarily previous to it.

3. Or, if we hold fast, "Other foundation can no man lay than that which is laid, even Jesus Christ"; and, "I am justified freely by God's grace, through the redemption which is in Jesus"; yet he will not cease to urge, "But the tree is known by its fruits. Have you the fruits of justification? Is that mind in you which was in Christ Jesus? Are you dead unto sin, and alive unto righteousness? Are you made conformable to the death of Christ, and do you know the power of His resurrection?" And then, comparing the small fruits we feel in our souls with the fullness of the promises, we shall be ready to conclude, "Surely God hath not said

that my sins are forgiven me! Surely I have not received the remission of my sins for what lot have I among them that are sanctified?"

4. More especially in the time of sickness and pain, he will press this with all his might: "Is it not the word of Him that cannot lie, 'Without holiness no man shall see the Lord'? But you are not holy; you know it well; you know holiness is the full image of God; and how far is this above, out of your sight? You cannot attain unto it. Therefore, all your labor has been in vain. All these things you have suffered in vain. You have spent your strength for nought. You are yet in your sins, and must therefore perish at the last." And thus, if your eye be not steadily fixed on Him who hath borne all your sins, he will bring you again under that "fear of death," whereby you were so long "subject unto bondage," and, by this means, impair, if not wholly destroy, your peace, as well as joy in the Lord.

5. But his master piece of subtilty is still behind. Not content to strike at your peace and joy, he will carry his attempts farther yet. He will level his assault against your righteousness also. He will endeavor to shake, yea, if it be possible, to destroy, the holiness you have already received, by your very expectation of receiving more, of attaining all the image of God.

6. The manner wherein he attempts this may partly appear from what has been already observed. For, First, by striking at our joy in the Lord, he strikes likewise at our holiness. Seeing joy in the Holy Spirit is a precious means of promoting every holy temper; a choice instrument of God, whereby he carries on much of his work in a believing soul. And it is a considerable help, not only to inward, but also to outward, holiness. It strengthens our hands to go on in the work of faith, and in the labor of love; manfully to "fight the good fight of faith and to lay hold on eternal life." It is peculiarly designed of God to be a balance both against inward and outward sufferings; to "lift up the hands that hang down, and confirm the feeble knees." Consequently, whatever damps our joy in the Lord, proportionably obstructs our holiness. And therefore, so far as Satan shakes our joy, he hinders our holiness also.

7. The same effect will ensue, if he can, by any means, either destroy or shake our peace for the peace of God is another precious means of advancing the image of God in us. There is scarce a greater help to holiness than this, a continual tranquillity of spirit, the evenness of a mind stayed upon God, a calm repose in the blood of Jesus. And without this, it is scarce possible to "grow in grace," and in the vital "knowledge of our Lord Jesus Christ." For all fear (unless the tender, filial fear) freezes and benumbs the soul. It binds up all the springs of spiritual life and stops all motion of the heart toward God. And doubt, as it were, bemires the soul, so that it sticks fast in the deep clay. Therefore, in the same proportion as either of these prevail, our growth in holiness is hindered.

8. At the same time that our wise adversary endeavors to make our conviction of the necessity of perfect love an occasion of shaking our peace by doubts and fears, he endeavors to weaken, if not destroy, our faith. Indeed these are inseparably connected so that they must stand or fall together. So long as faith subsists, we remain in peace; our heart stands fast while it believes in the Lord. But if we let go our faith, our filial confidence in a loving, pardoning God, our peace is at an end, the very foundation on which it stood being overthrown. And this is the only foundation of holiness as well as of peace; consequently, whatever strikes at this, strikes at the very root of all holiness. For without this faith, without an abiding sense that Christ loved me, and gave Himself for me, without a continuing conviction that God for Christ's sake is merciful to me a sinner, it is impossible that I should love God. "We love him, because he first loved us"; and we love Him in proportion to the strength and clearness of our conviction that He has loved us and accepted us in His Son. And unless we love God, it is not possible that we should love our neighbor as ourselves; nor, consequently, that we should have any right affections, either toward God, or toward man. It evidently follows that whatever weakens our faith must, in the same degree, obstruct our holiness. And this is not only the most effectual, but also the most compendious, way of destroying all holiness, see-

ing it does not affect any one Christian temper, any single grace or fruit of the Spirit, but, so far as it succeeds, tears up the very root of the whole work of God.

9. No marvel, therefore, that the ruler of the darkness of this world should here put forth all his strength. And so we find by experience. For it is far easier to conceive, than it is to express, the unspeakable violence wherewith this temptation is frequently urged on them who hunger and thirst after righteousness. When they see in a strong and clear light on the one hand, the desperate wickedness of their own hearts—on the other hand, the unspotted holiness to which they are called in Christ Jesus; on the one hand, the depth of their own corruption, of their total alienation from God—on the other, the height of the glory of God, that image of the Holy One wherein they are to be renewed; there is, many times, no spirit left in them; they could almost cry out, "With God this is impossible!" They are ready to give up both faith and hope; to cast away that very confidence whereby they are to overcome all things through Christ strengthening them and whereby, "after they have done the will of God," they are to "receive the promise."

10. And if they "hold fast the beginning of their confidence steadfast unto the end," they shall undoubtedly receive the promise of God reaching through both time and eternity. But here is another snare laid for our feet. While we earnestly pant for that part of the promise which is to be accomplished here "for the glorious liberty of the children of God," we may be led unawares from the consideration of the glory which shall hereafter be revealed. Our eye may be insensibly turned aside from that crown which the righteous Judge has promised to give at that day "to all that love his appearing"; and we may be drawn away from the view of that incorruptible inheritance which is reserved in heaven for us. But this also would be a loss to our souls and an obstruction to our holiness. For to walk in the continual sight of our goal is a needful help in our running the race that is set before us. This it was, the having "respect unto the recompense of the reward," which, of old time, encouraged Moses rather "to suffer affliction

with the people of God, than to enjoy the pleasures of sin for a season; esteeming the reproach of Christ greater riches than the treasures of Egypt." Nay, it is expressly said of a greater than he, that, "for the joy that was set before him, he endured the cross, and despised the shame," till He "sat down at the right hand of the throne of God." Whence we may easily infer how much more needful for us is the view of that joy set before us that we may endure whatever cross the wisdom of God lays upon us, and press on through holiness to glory.

11. But while we are reaching to this, as well as to that glorious liberty which is preparatory to it, we may be in danger of falling into another snare of the devil wherein he labors to entangle the children of God. We may take too much thought for tomorrow so as to neglect the improvement of today. We may so expect perfect love, as not to use that which is already shed abroad in our hearts. There have not been wanting instances of those who have greatly suffered hereby. They were so taken up with what they were to receive hereafter, as utterly to neglect what they had already received. In expectation of having five talents more, they buried their one talent in the earth. At least, they did not improve it as they might have done, to the glory of God, and the good of their own souls.

12. Thus does the subtle adversary of God and man endeavor to make void the counsel of God, by dividing the gospel against itself, and making one part of it overthrow the other while the first work of God in the soul is destroyed by the expectation of His perfect work. We have seen several of the ways wherein he attempts this by cutting off, as it were, the springs of holiness. But this he likewise does more directly by making that blessed hope an occasion of unholy tempers.

13. Thus, whenever our heart is eagerly athirst for all the great and precious promises, when we pant after the fullness of God as the hart after the waterbrook, when our soul breaks out in fervent desire, "Why are His chariot-wheels so long a-coming?"—he will not neglect the opportunity of tempting us to murmur against God. He will use all his wisdom, and all his

strength, if haply, in an unguarded hour, we may be influenced to repine at our Lord for thus delaying His coming. At least, he will labor to excite some degree of fretfulness or impatience and, perhaps, of envy at those whom we believe to have already attained the prize of our high calling. He well knows that by giving way to any of these tempers, we are pulling down the very thing we would build up. By thus following after perfect holiness, we become more unholy than before. Yea, there is great danger that our last state should be worse than the first; like them of whom the Apostle speaks in those dreadful words, "It had been better for them not to have known the way of righteousness, than, after they have known it, to turn from the holy commandment delivered to them."

14. And from hence he hopes to reap another advantage, even to bring up an evil report of the good way. He is sensible, how few are able to distinguish (and too many are not willing so to do) between the accidental abuse, and the natural tendency, of a doctrine. These, therefore, will he continually blend together with regard to the doctrine of Christian perfection in order to prejudice the minds of unwary men against the glorious promises of God. And how frequently, how generally, I had almost said how universally, has he prevailed herein! For who is there that observes any of these accidental ill effects of this doctrine and does not immediately conclude this is its natural tendency; and does not readily cry out, "See, these are the fruits (meaning the natural, necessary fruits) of such doctrine"? Not so. They are fruits which may accidentally spring from the abuse of a great and precious truth. But the abuse of this, or any other scriptural doctrine, does by no means destroy its use. Neither can the unfaithfulness of man, perverting his right way, make the promise of God of no effect. No, let God be true, and every man a liar. The Word of the Lord, it shall stand. "Faithful is he that hath promised: He also will do it." Let not us then be "removed from the hope of the Gospel." Rather let us observe, which was the Second thing proposed, how we may retort these fiery darts of the wicked

one, how we may rise the higher by what he intends for an occasion of our falling.

II. How Satan Works

1. Does Satan endeavor to damp our joy in the Lord by the consideration of our sinfulness, and then add to this that without entire, universal holiness, no man can see the Lord? You may cast back this dart upon his own head, while, through the grace of God, the more you feel of your own vileness, the more you rejoice in the confident hope that all this shall be done away. While you hold fast this hope, every evil temper you feel, though you hate it with a perfect hatred, may be a means, not of lessening your humble joy, but rather of increasing it. "This and this," may you say, "shall likewise perish from the presence of the Lord. Like as the wax melteth at the fire, so shall this melt away before his face." By this means, the greater that change is which remains to be wrought in your soul, the more may you triumph in the Lord and rejoice in the God of your salvation who has done so great things for you already, and will do so much greater things than these.

2. The more vehemently he assaults your peace with that suggestion, "God is holy; you are unholy; you are immensely distant from that holiness without which you cannot see God. How then can you be in the favor of God? How can you fancy you are justified?" Take the more earnest heed to hold fast that, "Not by works of righteousness which I have done, I am found in him; I am accepted in the Beloved; not having my own righteousness, (as the cause, either in whole or in part, of our justification before God,) but that which is by faith in Christ, the righteousness which is of God by faith." O bind this about your neck. Write it upon the table of your heart. Wear it as a bracelet upon your arm, as frontlets between your eyes. "I am justified freely by his grace through the redemption that is in Jesus Christ." Value and esteem, more and more, that precious truth, "By grace we are saved through faith." Admire, more and more, the free grace of God in so loving the world as to give "his only begotten Son, that whosoever believeth in him might not perish, but have everlasting

life." So shall the sense of the sinfulness you feel, on the one hand, and of the holiness you expect, on the other, both contribute to establish your peace and to make it flow as a river. So shall that peace flow on with an even stream in spite of all those mountains of ungodliness which shall become a plain in the day when the Lord comes to take full possession of your heart. Neither will sickness, or pain, or the approach of death occasion any doubt or fear. You know a day, an hour, a moment, with God is as a thousand years. He cannot be straitened for time wherein to work whatever remains to be done in your soul. And God's time is always the best time. Therefore be careful for nothing; only make your requests known unto Him and that not with doubt or fear, but thanksgiving, as being previously assured. He cannot withhold from you any manner of thing that is good.

3. The more you are tempted to give up your shield, to cast away your faith, your confidence in His love, so much the more take heed that you hold fast that whereunto you have attained; so much the more labor to stir up the gift of God which is in you. Never let that slip. "I have 'an Advocate with the Father, Jesus Christ the righteous'; and, 'The life I now live, I live by faith in the Son of God, who loved me, and gave himself for me.'" Be this your glory and crown of rejoicing; and see that no one take your crown. Hold that fast: "I know that my Redeemer liveth, and shall stand at the latter day upon the earth"; and, "I now 'have redemption in his blood, even the forgiveness of sins.'" Thus, being filled with all peace and joy in believing, press on, in the peace and joy of faith, to the renewal of your whole soul in the image of Him who created you!

Meanwhile, cry continually to God, that you may see the prize of your high calling, not as Satan represents it, in a horrid dreadful shape, but in its genuine native beauty; not as something that *must* be, or you will go to hell, but as what *may* be, to lead you to heaven. Look upon it as the most desirable gift which is in all the stores of the rich mercies of God. Beholding it in this true point of light, you will hunger after it more and more; your whole soul will be

athirst for God and for this glorious conformity to His likeness; and, having received a good hope of this and strong
consolation through grace, you will no more be weary or
faint in your mind, but will follow on till you attain.

4. In the same power of faith, press on to glory. Indeed,
this is the same prospect still. God has joined, from the
beginning, pardon, holiness, heaven. And why should man
put them asunder? O beware of this! Let not one link of the
golden chain be broken. "God, for Christ's sake, has forgiv-
en me. He is now renewing me in His own image. Shortly
He will make me meet for Himself, and take me to stand
before His face. I, whom He has justified through the blood
of His Son, being thoroughly sanctified by His Spirit, shall
quickly ascend to the 'New Jerusalem, the city of the living
God.' Yet a little while, and I shall 'come to the general
assembly and church of the first-born, and to God the Judge
of all, and to Jesus the Mediator of the New Covenant.'
How soon will these shadows flee away, and the day of
eternity dawn upon me! How soon shall I drink of 'the river
of the water of life, going out of the throne of God and of the
Lamb! There all His servants shall praise Him, and shall
see His face, and His name shall be upon their foreheads.
And no night shall be there; and they have no need of a
candle, or the light of the sun. For the Lord God enlightens
them, and they shall reign forever and ever.'"

5. And if you thus "taste of the good word, and of the
powers of the world to come," you will not murmur against
God because you are not yet "meet for the inheritance of
the saints in light." Instead of repining at your not being
wholly delivered, you will praise God for thus far delivering
you. You will magnify God for what He has done, and take
it as an earnest of what He will do. You will not fret
against Him because you are not yet renewed, but bless
Him because you shall be and because "now is your salvation" from all sin "nearer than when you" first "believed."
Instead of uselessly tormenting yourself because the time
is not fully come, you will calmly and quietly wait for it,
knowing that it "will come, and will not tarry." You may,
therefore, the more cheerfully endure, as yet, the burden of
sin that still remains in you because it will not always

remain. Yet a little while and it shall be clean gone. Only "tarry thou the Lord's leisure." Be strong, and "he shall comfort thy heart"; and put your trust in the Lord!

6. And if you see any who appear to be already partakers of their hope, already "made perfect in love"; far from envying the grace of God in them, let it rejoice and comfort your heart. Glorify God for their sake! "If one member is honored," shall not "all the members rejoice with it"? Instead of jealously or evil surmising concerning them, praise God for the consolation! Rejoice in having a fresh proof of the faithfulness of God in fulfilling all His promises; and stir yourself up the more to serve Christ Jesus!"

7. In order to do this, redeem the time. Improve the present moment. Buy up every opportunity of growing in grace or of doing good. Let not the thought of receiving more grace tomorrow make you negligent of today. You have one talent now. If you expect five more, so much the rather improve what you have. And the more you expect to receive hereafter, the more labor for God now. Sufficient for the day is the grace thereof. God is now pouring His benefits upon you. Now approve yourself a faithful steward of the present grace of God. Whatever may be tomorrow, give all diligence today, to "add to your faith courage, temperance, patience, brotherly-kindness," and the fear of God, till you attain that pure and perfect love! Let these things be now "in you and abound!" Be not now slothful or unfruitful. "So shall an entrance be ministered unto you into the everlasting kingdom of our Lord Jesus Christ!"

8. Lastly, if in time past you have abused this blessed hope of being holy as He is holy, yet do not therefore cast it away. Let the abuse cease, the use remain. Use it now to the more abundant glory of God and profit of your soul. In steadfast faith, in calm tranquillity of spirit, in full assurance of hope, rejoicing evermore for what God has done, press on unto perfection! Grow daily in the knowledge of our Lord Jesus Christ, and go on from strength to strength, in resignation, patience, and humble thankfulness for what you have attained, and for what you shall attain. Run the race set before you, "looking unto Jesus," till, through perfect love, you enter into His glory!